How to pray so that God listens

By Zehra Mahoon

Copyright © 2016 by Zehra Mahoon. All Rights Reserved.

No part of this publication may be reproduced, distributed, or transmitted in any form or by any means, including photocopying, recording, or other electronic or mechanical methods, or by any information storage and retrieval system without the prior written permission of the publisher, except in the case of very brief quotations embodied in critical reviews and certain other non-commercial uses permitted by copyright law.

The author of this book does not dispense any form of medical or psychological advice or prescribe the use of any technique as a form of treatment for physical, emotional, or medical problems without the advice of a physician, either directly or indirectly. The intent of the author is to offer information of a general nature to help you in your search for emotional and spiritual well-being. If you apply any of the techniques offered in the book, the author and the publisher assume no responsibility for your actions.

*This book is dedicated to my mother Zarina Mahoon.
Much of what I know of life and living is because of her.*

Zehra

Table of Contents

Why I wrote this book 1
Why you should read this book 5
Understanding prayer 1
Living life from a place of God consciousness 11
The six thinking choices 17
The role of trust and faith 22
The prayer process..25
How to use the prayers contained in this book 29
A practical example of how to use the prayers 31
One Hundred Prayers 41
Abraham's morning intention.. 349
About the author 350

How to pray so that God listens...

By Zehra Mahoon

Prayer is not a spare
wheel that you pull out
when in trouble;
it is a steering wheel
that directs the right
path throughout life

~Annonymous~

Why I wrote this book

One day many years ago I came upon my mother sobbing her heart out. I hugged her and asked her what was wrong. She said she had been praying and that was why she was crying. I didn't understand. "Why is praying making you cry?" I asked her. She said "because I am praying from the bottom of my heart". And then she said something that has been with me forever, it has been at the heart of my search for God. She said, "all prayers are not the same, you have to pray so that God listens".

At the time, I interpreted it to mean that you have to pray from the bottom of your heart. But as I saw my mother's life unfold, I knew that there was more to the mix. She always prayed from the bottom of her heart; often she sobbed real hard but her life was tough and she was mostly a very unhappy person, and I knew that very few of her prayers were answered. I could not understand it. Why did God not grant her wishes? What was she doing wrong? My mother lived by the book – she always tried really hard to do the right thing. She always put others before herself and tried to keep everyone happy. She was a truly good person at heart and a truly miserable one.

As a child I wanted to be exactly like my mother as a person and so I learned to copy her – like a puppy I wanted to please her in any manner possible so I turned into a junior version of her. As an adult I wanted to be her opposite in creating my life. I did not want my life to be as empty of joy as hers. She propelled me to investigate and seek why things happened the way they did. I thought that there was no one more deserving of joy than my mother and it perplexed me that it was so hard to convince God to respond to her pleas. My mother engaged in vigils and I engaged in them with her, together we practiced many days of prayer and abstinence, trying to please God so that our prayers would be answered but mostly to no avail. From all of it, I came away with a deep-seated knowing that my mother was right: "all prayers are not the same, you have to pray so that God listens".

My quest came to an end when I understood God's system for granting wishes. Really, it is a very simple system.

The reason we don't understand it is because it is not based on human logic, but on emotional logic. We humans look for the logic in the way things happen, and so often we completely miss the point.

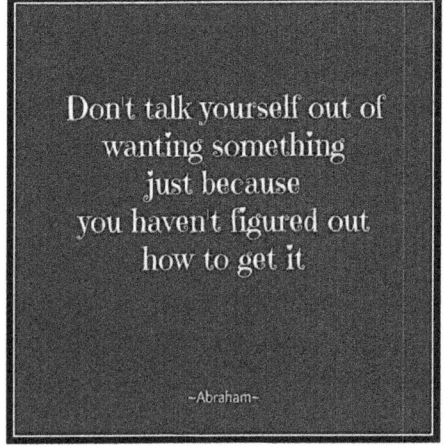

God does not respond to our logical arguments, God responds to our emotional frequency. When we tune ourselves to the frequency of love, God responds and the doors of heaven open to release all that our hearts desire and more. It's as simple as that. Logic complicates it, because we look around us at the complexity of nature and surmise that God's system must be complicated. We look around us at the scores of people living mundane unenjoyable lives and conclude that there must be something elusive in the mix that makes God answer prayers. However, it is true:

All prayers are answered.

We just don't know that we are praying – we think we are thinking, but all thoughts are prayers and God not only listens to each one, but also responds to each one.

When we think (and therefore offer prayer) from any other frequency aside from love, we get less than what we want. In the daily hustle and bustle of life, we humans have forgotten how to be in love. In love with the world, in love with our selves, in love with others, in love with our lives, and there-in lies the problem; for until we tune our selves to the frequency of love we cannot receive the station from which God is transmitting the guidance that we need in order to live happy and completely fulfilled lives.

So dear friends, those who are reading these words – this book is written for you. It is my way of giving back, my way of spreading joy, my way of helping, my way of contributing to the knowledge of this world. In this book, I am sharing with you what I know about "how to pray so that God listens". But my most precious gift to you is the collection of prayers to start your day with. Just open the book to whatever page calls you in the morning and read the prayer that it contains. If you feel like taking it a step further grab a paper and pen and continue the prayer in your own way, in your own words.

Once you know how to structure your thoughts into a deliberate string comprising a prayer that is emitted on the frequency of love, you will gain confidence and power. Confidence in knowing that all prayers are answered and power in being able to control the outcomes in your life. **All prayers are answered, all wishes are granted.** If they don't show up in our lives, it has to do with our ability to allow them in. Change the way you think about the process of prayer. The purpose of prayer is not to tell God what you want, but to bring yourself into a state of allowing all good things to come to you.

> If the only prayer you said was thank you, that would be enough
>
> ~Meister Eckhart~

Why you should read this book

You should read this book if, like me, you have been seeking answers to the questions below:

- What is a prayer?
- Is prayer a useless ritual?
- Why should I pray?
- Will I get all the things I want if I pray?
- Is there a right and wrong way to pray?
- Does God answer all prayers?
- Why do people who never pray get what they want, and those who pray don't?
- What does 'Ask and it is Given' really mean?
- What should a prayer include?
- Is there a good or bad time to pray?
- Why are some prayers answered quickly and others take a long time?
- Why do some people get everything they want and others don't?
- Does religion make a difference to the effectiveness of prayer?
- Is God really fair?
- Does God really love me?
- Why do bad things happen to good people?
- Can I really put my trust in God?
- Can I control the outcomes in my life?
- Can I improve my life and be truly happy?
- Can I truly have, be and do anything I want?

These and many other questions are answered in these pages.

I had been asking these questions for a very long time, and then I met Abraham, my teacher and my guide, and my life started changing little by little, until one day I woke up and realized that everything had changed for the better. Since then, I have found peace within and a knowing that things always work out. That there is always a way, and that I don't need to know what it is or how to find it.

I am not the only teacher who is teaching this stuff. But I believe I have my own unique way of explaining what I have learnt and that there are many who will "get it" because my way of explaining and teaching resonates with them.

I trust that if you are here, reading this now, then you are ready for what is contained in these pages, and there is no doubt that it will help you on your journey.

We really are all in this together.
Zehra

How to pray so that God listens

By Zehra Mahoon

Every thought is a prayer
And every prayer is answered

~Zehra Mahoon~

Understanding prayer

I've asked a lot of questions. Ever since I can remember, I have observed disparity between what I was taught about how things should work and how they actually worked. And so I have been seeking answers. I have been seeking information that would explain why. The biggest question in my mind was why did those people succeed who did not play by the rules of religion and society – they did not pray; they did not observe any of the rituals we were supposed to do to win God over, they were not nice to others and yet they were happier than people like my mother, who always followed all the rituals, prayed devotedly and always made an effort to do what others thought was right.

I feel truly blessed to have found the answers to all my questions, and to have found a framework for explaining everything in life. God's system is really simple and easy to understand. It was not that easy to practice in the beginning, but that was mainly because I wasn't used to it, and I didn't quite understand all its nuances. With practice it becomes easy; it becomes the way you live life and think your thoughts and respond to the world around you, and then life takes on a magical quality where you feel completely at peace. It is a good place to be.

Here are some of the questions I have asked, along with the answers I have found.

Why do we pray? What is a prayer?

We pray because we believe that there is an entity outside of us that controls what happens to us. We pray because we believe we have to communicate what we want to this entity, so that it can act on our behalf and make those things possible for us that we want but do not know how to get. We believe that this entity has ultimate power over all things in the universe and can make all things possible. We call this entity God.

We believe that God knows everything, and yet we feel we need to tell God what we want. I always used to wonder about that. Shouldn't the all-knowing, all-powerful God already know what was in my heart, and what I was thinking?

The answer is: God does know. In fact, that which we call God is aware of every thought we think. Yes, each and every thought. Nothing escapes God. And we never have to make prayer a special ritual because God is listening all the time, not just at the time when we kneel or sit on a prayer mat. Therefore, we need to be aware of how we think all our thoughts, not just the ones we offer during the period of time we label as prayer.

Every little thought we think contributes to how our life unfolds.

Every thought is a prayer.

Every thought we think is a communication with God. And our emotional response to the thoughts we think is our guidance system telling us whether we are thinking in a manner that is on track with how God wants us to behave or not. When we feel good, we are on track and when we feel bad we are not on track.

You see, God always responds to all our thoughts and prayers; we on the other hand are not always listening. Our heads are always busy thinking and so even though God is calling us towards what we need to do in order to get what we want – we aren't listening. It's as if God were trying to get a word in but we were talking so fast that we ignored the signals and did not stop to listen. Ever heard that proverb: "when your mouth is open, your ears are closed"?

So how does this system of communication with God really work?

Just for a moment, imagine that we have a walkie-talkie which we can use to communicate with God. Imagine also that God responds to us on the same frequency that we "choose" to communicate on. These communication frequencies correspond to the emotions we feel. When we feel good we transmit and receive on the frequency of love and joy. God responds on the same frequency. When we transmit from a frequency of sadness, anger or worry, we receive on that frequency as well. God always reflects back to us the frequency on which we are tuned. The life that we live is a reflection of how we are tuned. The closer we are tuned to love and joy, the happier we are in life.

God is love, and when we feel the emotion of love we are on the same frequency as God. All good things are transmitted on this frequency. Emotions that feel good are emotions we call love, joy, hope, satisfaction, eagerness etc.

When we tune our walkie-talkie to negative emotions; emotions that feel bad such as worry, anxiety, frustration, anger, blame, guilt or despair, we start transmitting our thoughts, and our prayers to God on this frequency. God listens to those prayers too but nothing good can be transmitted back to us from God on this frequency, because when you transmit on the frequency of anger, you cannot receive that which is being transmitted on the frequency of joy. *Ask and it is Given.* But it is always given on the frequency of love and joy and when you are not feeling those emotions you cannot Receive. All prayers are answered – every time, but we have to be in a place of receiving what is being sent out way. The beauty of God's system is that God's transmission never stops, and as soon as we stop complaining and tune ourselves to love we receive everything that was being transmitted for us from the moment that we asked.

We are good at asking but many of us have forgotten how to receive. That's Ok because God sent us into the world equipped with a system that always lets us know whether we are tuned to the Receiving mode or not. That system is our capacity to feel; it is our intuition. When the thought of something makes us feel a negative emotion – it's a clue that tells us that we are not looking at things the way that God is looking at them from a vantage point of love and joy.

Another clue is contained in the life we are living. If we have the things we have asked for then that is proof that we have been good at tuning ourselves to the frequency of love and joy – the frequency of God, the frequency of Receiving. And if there is a pre-dominant absence in our lives of the things we want to live, then it means that we have been transmitting and receiving on a frequency that is lower than the frequency of Receiving. So everything we receive while we are on a negative frequency falls short of what we truly want. When you stub your toe, and then spill coffee all over your new sweater, and chip a nail that catches in the new sweater, you know that you are thinking thoughts that do not serve you – you are not on a frequency of love and appreciation. Most of us crib and complain and say things like "Oh God, it's one of those days…", but what we really need to do at that time is to stop and say, "Obviously I am tuned to the wrong frequency. I need to shift my attention – what can I think of just now that I am grateful for in my life?" and then turn our attention to that.

You see, God wants us to be in a state of love and joy so that we can receive those things that will bring us more love and joy. When we say "God, grant me this wish 'so that' I can be happy", God responds by saying "Be happy, my child, and then your wish will be granted". And that, my dear friends, is the secret to prayer. You have to think and pray from a place of love and joy and then all your prayers will be answered the way you want them to be answered. Prayer is all about the concept of "Praise" and "Grace".

When we feel negative emotion of any sort, our guidance system is telling us that we are not transmitting our thoughts and prayers on the frequency of love and joy, on the frequency that brings us the results we want to experience and therefore it calls our attention towards the work we need to do in order to shift our emotional state to a place of love and joy. If we persist in a place of complaining about our circumstances, telling others about it, feeling jealous that others have what we want, feeling angry with the world in general and even ourselves, we stay in a place where life feels hard and things take more time than they would otherwise.

The bottom line is: we must feel good in order for good things to happen, and not wait for good things to happen so that we can feel good.

> You can tell what you are ready for by what's coming. Because if you're not ready, it's not coming.
>
> ~Abraham~

Have you ever been in a place where you asked "why me?", or "what did I do to deserve this?" I have, and now I know better. I know now that it was my attention to such thoughts that kept good things from coming to me. I was praying really hard for my life to improve, but I was doing it all on a communication frequency on which I could not receive the things I wanted. God's system is completely fair --it gives those who complain more to complain about and it gives those who appreciate more to be appreciative about.

We use the same philosophy with children when we refuse to give in to the tantrums they throw when they ask for a candy. We tell them they have to be nice and say please and thank you. We don't give in to their tantrums and their tears. In the same way, when we pray from a place of despair, we are not asking with a please and thank you. Instead, if we start with saying thank you Dear God... thank you for this, and this and this. Thank you for so and so, and thank you for that, and that and that... and by the way please may I have this thing I want. That's how to pray so that God listens.

You see, when we appreciate the things we already have it makes us feel abundance in our life. We feel good, and when we ask for more on that frequency of feeling good, God responds by sending us more things to feel good about. When we kick up a fuss, point fingers at others and throw tantrums, God system responds by sending us more stuff that corresponds to the way we feel. These things that happen to us are supposed to be indicators that tell us that we are not on the frequency of love.

Imagine this: little Tommy goes up to his mommy and hugs her. Then he puts on his best smile and says "Mommy I love you, you are the best mommy in the world". Mummy looks at him with doting eyes, and then little Tommy says "Mommy may I please have a piece of cake? It looks delicious and I love how it smells, and I'm so happy that you brought it home, I am sure I will love it when I eat it, thank you, thank you, thank you". Mummy says "Well Tommy, you are such a good little boy, of course you can have some cake".

Take another example: little Timmy goes up to his mommy and stomps his feet "Why are you so horrible to me? There is cake in the house and you haven't given me any, why can't I have cake? I've been asking for it for so long. Tommy got cake and I didn't, he always gets everything he wants, and I've been asking for a very long time. I don't think you love me – my life is miserable". His mother responds by saying "Timmy, we love you, and you have so many good things already. You should be grateful; there are so many children in the world who would love to be in your shoes. Be good, change your attitude and then you can have all the cake you want". Timmy throws a tantrum "I never get anything I want". He sobs and cries, but his mother doesn't give in. Because if she did, then she would not be fair to all her other children. She has to be consistent in her response in order to be fair to all her children, otherwise she would be playing favourites and her children would never know for sure what to do in order to get cake.

God is like that. God does not play favourites. God's system is consistent and it is fair. You can count on it to work the same way every time for every one of God's children.

One thing that is different about God's love compared to us humans is that God holds love as a constant. It doesn't matter how we behave, God never stops loving us. As soon as we change our attitude and make peace with where we are and start appreciating all the good in our lives, we start receiving things that we have been wanting. The fact that we feel negative emotions is because we are not on the frequency of love. That feeling is telling us that we need to change our perspective; that we are not thinking thoughts that serve us, that we need to start thinking in a manner that is conducive to feeling good. All we need to do is to get on the frequency of love for things to start changing, and we do that by thinking thoughts that feel better, thoughts that distract us from our unhappiness and direct our attention towards something that feels better.

This is why we see examples of people who never pray and are not at all religious get what they want. You see it is about being happy, not about the ritual of prayer. The happier we are the more we receive and the happier still we become. The unhappier we are the unhappier we get – unless we make a conscious effort to break the cycle. This is why bad things can happen to good people. Because being good in the way society labels people as good or bad is not the basis on which prayers are answered.

What we transmit is what we receive. For centuries we have called this "karma", for eons we have passed down through the generations the words: "what you sow is what you reap" and what "goes around, comes around". Every stage of humandom has known how the universe works and how prayers are answered, and every generation has used its own methods to pass down this information – no wonder it becomes like the Chinese whisper, losing the true message somewhere along the way. Philosophers and poets show up, and prophets from time to time, all asking questions until they go deep enough to start receiving the answers directly from God. But really each one of us has the ability to do so ourselves, for each one of us has the ability to love.

The gist of it is that when we live life from a place of love for everything and everyone we attain a state of God consciousness or ascension from which all things are possible.

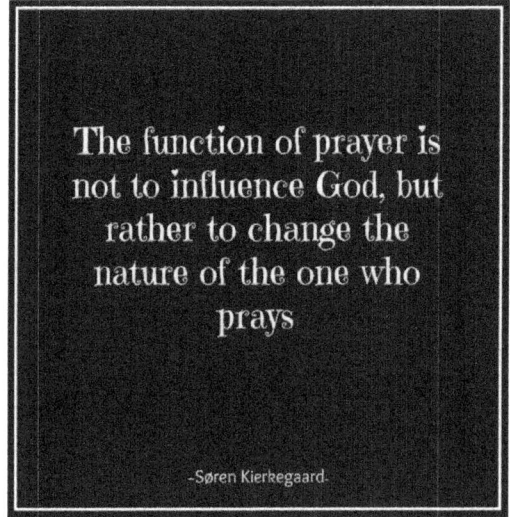

Living life from a place of God consciousness

Perception is a choice.

In every moment we make the decision to see things the way we choose to see them. We can decide to take ownership for our role in what is happening in our life or we can decide to feel powerless and at the mercy of external forces. We can decide to love or not. We can decide what to pay attention to and what to ignore. What we pay attention to expands and occupies a bigger place in our lives, and what we choose to ignore diminishes. Isn't that why we often make the choice to ignore behaviour that we don't want to encourage in our children?

Your neighbour decides to dump garbage on your property – how will you react? You could think of a number of ways to get even. You could think of many instances in the past when your neighbour has behaved in ways you did not like. You can remind yourself of what other people have said about your neighbour. Or you could say to yourself "Ah... I am attracting an experience that I do not want. This means that my vibration is not aligned with the frequency of love. God is using my neighbour as a vehicle to communicate to me that I need to do something about the way I have been thinking – what can I turn my attention to in order to tune myself to the frequency of love? I think I will go and hug my cat and feel the love I feel for her." If you did this you would have tuned yourself closer to the frequency of love, and changed the direction of future events in your life.

Your partner or spouse is unpleasant to you one morning – how will you react? You could think "What's wrong with them? What did I do to deserve that? If you're having a bad day, don't take it out on others! Maybe they don't love me anymore, maybe this is an indication that there is something wrong in our relationship". On the other hand, you could think "Oh no… I must not be on the frequency of love in order to have drawn this experience to me… what can I think about to shift my emotional frequency… I can think about when we first met how much fun that was, we've shared some beautiful moments… I felt so blessed when I first met this person". And as you think these thoughts you rekindle the feeling of love that you felt in the past for this person, and just that much shift in the way you look at them takes you towards God consciousness. If you were to hate them, and keep boiling over what they said, and telling your best friend about it you would perpetuate the feeling of anger and that would result in your attracting more events, people and things from that place of negative frequency. Make sense? That's why the saying goes "the better it gets the better it gets". When you feel good, you think and act from a good feeling place and that brings more good things to feel good about.

It is widely accepted that acting from a place of anger does not bring good results. We have all heard it said, "let the anger subside before you act", because anger is a negative emotion. It is far away from the frequency of love and therefore, when you think and pray from a place of anger what happens next will just be proof of where you are emotionally. Proof that you need to change the way you are thinking your thoughts so that your life can change for the better.

What is truly unfortunate is that most of us have accepted a life of mediocrity because we have forgotten what the feeling of pure love feels like. We have forgotten the feeling of pure joy. So we live one day to the next not really knowing what to aim for. What is the feeling of true love and pure joy? We try to rekindle joy by buying new things, going out to eat and entertain – trying to fill a void in our lives through these things. All we really need to do is to close our eyes and think of something that makes us feel pure joy and then go shopping, and then go out to eat, and then meet with friends. Because when you put yourself on the frequency of love and joy before you do anything then the results of your action will be far more satisfying than otherwise.

Do you remember the love you felt for your child or grandchild when you first held them? Do you remember the love you felt for your kitten or your puppy when you first brought them home? Do you still feel that love when you think about them, and when you interact with them? Do you remember being swept off your feet by your true love? Do you still feel that way about them? Do you remember the joy of playing with a balloon, or blowing bubbles? Do you remember laughing because it was fun to laugh, and jumping and skipping because it was fun? Do you remember the excitement of opening presents on your Birthday? Can you connect with the feeling of pure love and pure joy? If you can work on remembering and if you can connect with those feelings "at will" without any change in your circumstances then you can reach a state of God consciousness literally overnight.

Your life can change for the better overnight.

If each one of us focused on changing our life by choosing to look at all things, people and events from a place of love, what a wonderful place this world would be. All of war is because of an absence of God consciousness, all pain and suffering is because of a lack of God consciousness – a lack of love. When we "choose" to look at our circumstances from a point of view that differs from God's view, we perpetuate a reality that is lacking the things we want.

You see, God always loves and sees perfection; when we hate we separate ourselves from God, whether that hate is directed at others or towards our own person – doesn't matter. When we find something wrong with a person or a situation we separate ourselves again. God always sees us as perfect and our circumstances as the perfect starting point for our journey going forward. God believes in our ability to tune ourselves to the frequency of love and joy at will in order to receive all the things our hearts desire – and that is why "when we ask, it is always given" – no exceptions.

When we start a journey going from one city to another and take the highway, we don't give up on the journey just because we hit a rough patch of road or road construction forces us to take a detour. We know that our destination exists and that if we persist "going forward" (as opposed to retracing our steps and going backwards), that we will eventually reach our destination. In life however, we forget this simple truth. When we set our sights on a goal and hit a rough patch we often give up on the goal itself. What complicates matters is that we tend to setup our goals in terms of physical manifestations, and when we don't get the specific manifestation that we desire we see ourselves as failures. That's going about it the wrong way. A much better way to setup goals and to ask God for things is to ask for how you want to feel and let God work out the details. For example, take the example of Mary. Dear Mary, madly in love with Harry. She thinks that there is no other man in the world who can make her as happy as she thinks she will be when she is together with Harry. So she makes herself unhappy by thinking about circumstances that have pulled her apart from Harry, and now she "decides" that she can never be happy again. Dear Mary is missing the point. What she is really asking for is happiness, and that happiness can come to her in so many different ways, it does not have to come to her by being with Harry. Her main goal is to find happiness with a mate. When she thinks about Harry, when she prays for Harry, she cannot help but notice that he's not there, and when she does that she cannot possibly be in a state of love and joy – she can't possibly say "I love Harry and I'm so glad things didn't work out for us and he's not there" and feel real joy inside her being. So every time she thinks or talks about this thing or person that she does not have she activates the emotion of lack – and that is not the frequency on which she can receive the true love and happiness that she wants to receive. Instead if she could bring herself to a place of feeling blessed because there are so many things in her life that are working, so many things to be appreciative about, so many things to give thanks for, then her heart would glow with the feeling of love and in that state of joy she could think "Dear God, please bring me together with a man who satisfies me at every level, and makes me feel the joy of co-creation" and let God figure out who that man will be she would receive what she wants much faster and with far more ease – and it could very well be Harry because now she is not thinking about him from an attitude of lack and she is putting her faith in God's power to bring her that which makes her happy.

When we hold our happiness back by making it conditional on something happening first, we cannot tune ourselves to the frequency of love and joy completely, and this is what pushes things we want away from us.

What we really need to do is to remember in every moment that we have six thinking choices and the choice we make determines what comes next.

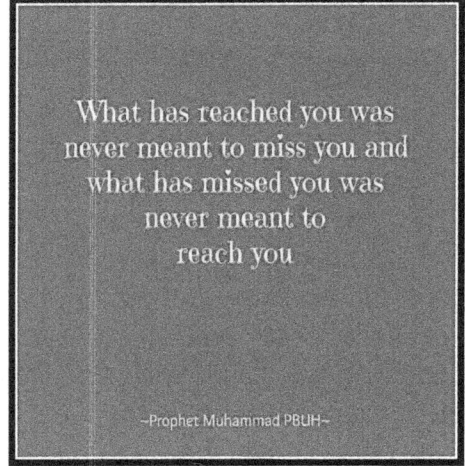

The six thinking choices

I first introduced the six thinking choices in the book "Thrive" and then in the book "Peace Within". The concept of the six thinking choices is at the base of all prayer. By exercising the ability to choose how we think we have the ability to tune ourselves to the frequency of love with ease and consistency. The basic premise is that in every moment we have a decision to make – the decision to pick a perspective or vantage point for thinking. We can chose to look at what has our attention from a point of view of finding ways to feel better and better or worse and worse.

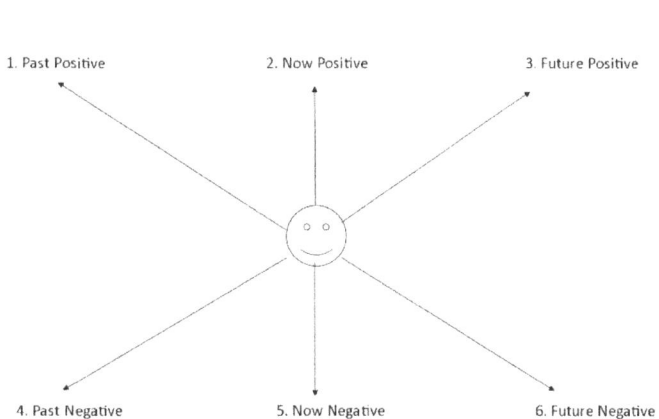

The above illustration has been reproduced from the book Peace Within by Zehra Mahoon.

For example, let's say Paul is looking for a job. He has the following six perspectives to pick from:

1. I've always had trouble getting what I want (past negative)
2. I can't see how things can change (future negative)
3. I don't have what it takes (now negative)
4. Sometimes unexpected good things can happen, I've seen that in the past (past positive)
5. There is no reason why the future can't be better than the past (future positive)
6. If other people can do it, I can too (now positive)

Which one of these choices he picks and repeats most often is what will determine how things unfold in his life. If the balance of his thought consists of the three positive choices then the chances of good things happening in his life, and not just on the job front are high, and vice versa. The amount of focus we give a thought converts it from a mere possibility to a probability, and if we continue to give it our attention then the probability becomes a certainty.

For the most part the way we think our thoughts is a habit. It gets formed the same way other habits get formed, like the habit we form about sleeping on one side of the bed, or sitting at a certain spot at the dinner table, or having a favourite chair near the TV. Similarly, we learn to look at the glass half full or half empty. This becomes our habitual perspective.

We learn perspective. Sometimes it's what we were taught, sometimes it's what we observed others do, and sometimes we learnt it on our own – it doesn't really matter how it came about. What matters is becoming conscious of the fact that when we use the first three thinking choices or perspectives we tune ourselves *away* from God consciousness and when we chose the last three we tune ourselves *toward* God consciousness.

At its base, being God conscious simply means looking at things, people and events the way God would look at them. When we know that God is love, and looks upon everyone with love, then it goes to reason that all we have to do in order to attain a place of God consciousness is to make love our anchor – to stay rooted in love no matter what; to look for the positive in everything past, present or future.

Simple everyday things reflect how we think. For example, two friends going to get pizza. One says to the other, "don't you just hate it when there isn't enough cheese?" "Yes," says the other, "and sometimes, one edge ends up being over done – I hate that – why can't they just get it right?" You'd think that this was a simple conversation about pizza, but every thought is a prayer. So with the words that these two friends are offering and the thoughts that they are thinking they are generating a negative vibration – they are focusing on what can go wrong instead of what has gone right in the past and can go well for them in the present. They think that their conversation is about pizza, but really their conversation is a reflection of their habit of thought. They are forgetting the countless times when they have had the perfect amount of cheese and the perfectly baked pizza and they are making the conscious choice of remembering the times when things did not go so well. As a result they have taken themselves off the frequency of God consciousness on which the perfect pizzas are cooked and served and other wonderful things happen.

A better way to have this conversation could be, "I absolutely love it when they put the perfect amount of cheese on it", and "Yes, and I love it when it is perfectly baked all around – in fact most of the time I enjoy perfectly baked pizza, and I am expecting another perfectly cooked, perfect tasting pizza again today". Do you see the difference in this conversation and the earlier one?

In the second conversation the two friends are positively anticipating--they are maintaining a positive stance about their past experiences, their present and their future and this makes a difference not only to the sort of pizza coming their way but also other things in life.

This is what is meant by the term "living in the now" – it's about finding a way to appreciate the present moment. The more we appreciate the more time we spend on the frequency of love.

There have been times in life when I have been so low emotionally, so hurt, that it is hard to find a thought that feels good. I have learnt that at times like that the best strategy is for me to get impersonal – to look for things outside of my own life and persona to find the positive, because looking at my own life just puts a magnifying glass on all the things I want that are missing. At such times I have found it useful to appreciate nature – the birds and the trees and the water, the flowers and the animals. It doesn't matter what is happening in your own life – you can still find something in nature to appreciate.

In summary, the six thinking choices help us to aim our focus on finding joy either in the past, in the present or by thinking of the future and as we do so we elevate our energy to that of love and joy and therefore to a state of God consciousness where all things that we want are possible. Remember that all prayers are answered, everything that we ask for is always given, we just have to bring ourselves to a place of receiving. So the function of prayer is not to tell God what we want, but to praise and be thankful so that we can bring ourselves to a place of receiving all that God is holding for us in trust.

> Your choices of action may be limited but your choices of thought are not
>
> ~Abraham~

The role of trust and faith

Have faith and put your trust in God. This seems to be a common theme across all religions. The idea of trusting God is an appealing one. It implies not having to worry about "how things will come about" and is based on the assumption that God is all knowing, and has power over all things. If we really believed this then there would be no place for worry in our lives because we would know with certainty that as we ask it is always given.

We are told to have blind faith, and that is an intellectually scary thought, which is why most us are unable to achieve blind faith. Unless you are someone who never worries, you do not have blind faith. But when you start understanding how God's system works, then faith no longer has to be blind and putting our trust in God is easy. Look at the world and everything in it from the perspective of God, the perspective of love, and you will never need blind faith.

When things don't work out the way you want them to, you know that it is an indication of the fact that you have been looking at things and thinking about them from a perspective that is less than that of love. And that is why we have complete responsibility for what happens to us in life. That is why we create our own reality – for God only gives us that for which we are ready. Demonstrate that you are ready for joy by practicing joy; demonstrate that you are ready for love by practicing love, demonstrate that you are ready for all good things by practicing feeling good, and then all those things that you want will find their way easily into your life.

One of the things that goes wrong with trust and faith is that many believers put their faith in God and then start looking for evidence that the things they are asking for are on their way, and when they start looking for evidence they negate the faith and trust that they were intending to abide by, so the things they want don't flow easily. There is no need to look for evidence. Instead tell yourself that you are looking forward to the ways in which God will surprise and delight you. Basically you look for evidence when you are not sure that what you have asked for is really on its way – that's doubt, and doubt is a negative emotion. You cannot receive things God is transmitting on the frequency of love when you are holding yourself in doubt or worry over them.

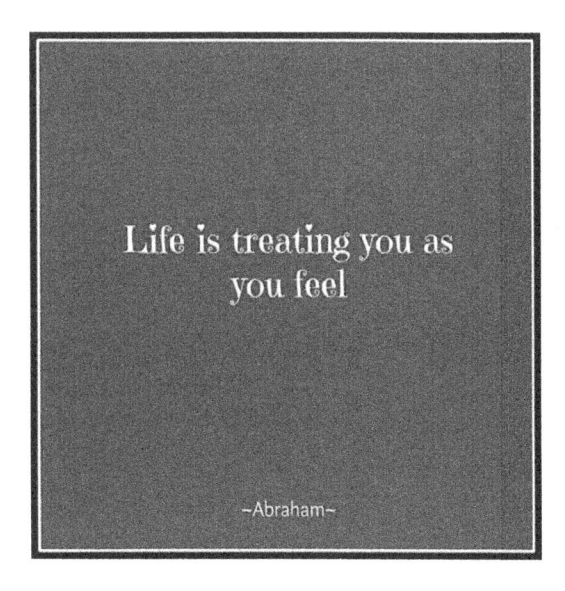

> Life is treating you as you feel
>
> ~Abraham~

At times when I find myself thinking about how things will come about and what the possibilities are, I remind myself that's not my job. I don't need to know how.

I've developed an analogy that helps me remember that I don't need to know. It goes like this:

Imagine that you have been given the opportunity to participate in a race. The prize for the winner is all the riches they want – unlimited wealth. All you have to do is to go across a deep, dense and dark forest without a map or compass and come out at the other end. This forest is known to be a dangerous place with many wild beasts, pitfalls and life-threatening terrain. You accept the challenge because you have a secret weapon that you know will give you the advantage you need in order to win. Your secret weapon is your best friend who is always there for you and never turns you down. Your best friend owns a helicopter and a set of walkie-talkies. You call your friend and ask them to help you navigate the forest from their aerial view, and with their help and guidance you are able to go across the forest in record time and win. That's the sort of thing we have going on with God. God can see everything and help us navigate the twists and turns of life easily. God can see a path where we think none exists. There is no need for us to question the path and where it leads. There is no need for us to ask, "Is this the right path? Will it lead me to where I want to go?" There is no question about it – God is always leading us towards our well-being, to that which is good for us, to that for which we are vibrationally, emotionally ready.

The prayer process

The bottom line is that the purpose of prayer is to elevate our vibrational frequency to meet God's. God is pure love, pure joy and when we feel the feeling of love, appreciation and joy we meet God.

Pray to feel good – not to make something happen so that you can feel good.

Trust and faith soothe us so that we can feel better in moments when doubt and other negative emotions sneak in. It is important not to judge yourself and your ability to connect with God because we all have that ability. The only reason we don't do it consistently is because we don't always hold on to trust and faith as our anchors.

I always gravitate towards the trees on our planet because to me they exemplify trust in the purest way. Trees stay rooted in their faith, trusting that after every winter there will be a summer and their leaves will return. Trees don't run around looking for food, they stay rooted in their faith, knowing that God will provide whatever they need. Trees share of themselves generously; they give their love in the form of their fruit, in the form of the shade they create, in the form of the wood they give us. Trees never turn anyone away. They don't mind death because they know that it is simply the cycle of life. The next time you worry or let doubt in, think about the trees and try to be one.

If you are someone who is mostly happy with your life, your persona, your relationships, your health and your financial situation, then it is certain that you must be thinking your thoughts mostly from a joyful place, because you are mostly receiving the things you have asked for. But if you are someone who has had a difficult life, and many of the things you have been asking for are still on their way then it is equally certain that you are getting in your own way by thinking thoughts in a manner that is not on the frequency of allowing – the frequency of love and joy on which God is transmitting. And if that is so, you have two alternatives: you can go cold turkey and shift your way of thinking in the blink of an eye – that's usually what we call an "awakening", or you can start becoming conscious of the way you think and what happens as a result and start shifting your thought process slowly, one step at a time, one day at a time by consciously using the six thinking choices, and by consciously focusing on things, people and circumstances from a point of view of love and appreciation.

As with learning any new skill the most important ingredient is consistency. If you keep at it, you will get it in the end. Just like learning to ride a bike, when you keep at it you eventually find your balance and away you go.

In summary, the prayer process is as follows:

1. Find things to appreciate – praise
2. Feel the feeling of appreciation and love at a visceral level in your body (not just lip service)

3. Generate positive energy so that you can hold yourself constant on the frequency of love and joy (use the six thinking choices)
4. Express your appreciation
5. Talk about how you want to feel rather than what you want to get
6. End your prayer at a high point while you are still feeling the feeling of high flying emotions
7. Let it be, don't start looking for specific results. Looking for evidence slows things down and that is what makes trust and having faith so important

Life changes when feelings change
Feelings change when thoughts change
Thoughts change when you pay attention to the way you think and feel

In the next section of this book, I have shared my morning prayer. I have found it most beneficial to wake up thinking of a word that I want to use at the centre of my prayer – a word that helps me to focus positively.

I have found it of immense value to share this word with a friend with whom I communicate many times during the course of the day, so that we each try to incorporate our word of the day in our conversation. This process has heightened my level of joy, however sharing is not necessary. Having a word of the day helps me to focus more keenly, however having a word of the day is not important. The only important thing is to appreciate, appreciate, appreciate. Appreciation, praise, and love are the keys that open the door and allow us to receive the bounty that God is always sending our way.

It gives me great joy to share my love and my joy with you, and it is my positive anticipation that the love and joy in your life will be magnified and multiplied manifold as a result of this sharing.

> A happy life is just a
> string of happy
> moments,
> but most people don't
> allow the happy moment
> because
> they are so busy trying
> to get a happy life
>
> ~Abraham~

How to use the prayers contained in this book

Any time is a good time to connect with God. God doesn't listen to us on a schedule. In fact, God is listening all the time. When we set aside time for prayer and meditation we are actually focusing consciously on lifting our vibrational frequency and holding it constant on the frequency of pure love. When we accomplish that state and do it consistently for a few minutes each day our life changes. We start feeling satisfaction speckled with joy and life just feels really really good.

You can read these payers at any time of the day and as many times as you like. There are no rules here.

I would love for you to start writing your own prayers. The process of writing a thought takes more time than speaking it out a loud. The process of speaking a thought out loud takes more time than the process of thinking it. When we write a prayer it keeps us in that pure positive place of love and joy for a lot longer compared to just thinking. What is most important is spending at least 15 minutes at a stretch in a state of appreciation for your life and things that you can observe and feel that ignite the feeling of love and joy inside you – that's all. Whether you write or speak or think, doesn't really matter. God is present all the time and a witness to all of it.

The best use of the prayers in this book is to use them as the starting point for what you want to achieve. These prayers are written from a general point of view with the intention of helping us get on the vibration of love and appreciation. Once you feel yourself on that frequency, you can add a few lines that are more specific to your life and situation and what you wish to achieve. In the next section, I will use one of the prayers from this book to illustrate how you can use these 100 prayers as your starting point, then add what you desire, and end at a place that still helps you to continue holding the vibration of love and appreciation.

You can start at one end of this book and go to the end or you can open the book to which ever page calls you on any particular day – it doesn't matter. All that matters is that you take the time to feel good.

There is much love here for you. May you thrive in every way. May your life be full of love and joy and may you spread that light all around you.

Zehra

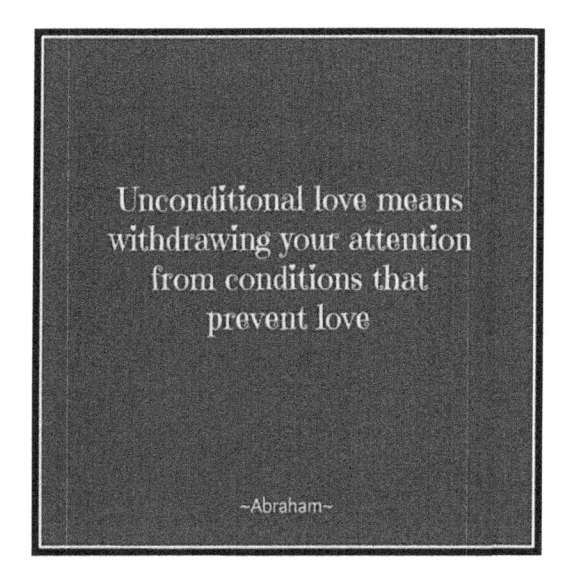

> Unconditional love means withdrawing your attention from conditions that prevent love
>
> ~Abraham~

A practical example of how to use the prayers

Reproduced here is one of my favourite prayers corresponding to the word "Ready". Where this prayer ends I have added a few lines to illustrate how you can ask for what you want. The important thing is to keep your frequency of love and appreciation steady.

Lets say the subject you wish to improve in your life is your **money situation** – here is an example of how you can ask for that while holding yourself steady.

Dear God, thank you for this beautiful brand new day
I feel ready to make the best of this day
I feel ready to enjoy every moment from waking up to going to bed
I feel ready to be happy
I feel ready to feel the energy of life around me and inside me
I feel ready to appreciate all the wonderful things I can see
I can see that the world is ready for me to enjoy
I can see that everything is always in the perfect place at the perfect time
I feel ready to explore new things today
I feel ready to receive abundance, freely flowing into my life
I feel ready to receive love and give love
I feel ready to feel the stamina and energy and the health of my physical body
I feel ready to appreciate myself and all the work I've done
I feel ready to appreciate who I am and who I am becoming
I feel ready to appreciate all those who have instigated my growth
I feel ready to appreciate the path that has helped me to the knowing that I now have
I feel ready to go with the ease and flow of life

I feel ready to take the path of least resistance
I feel ready to trust and allow You to Guide me to my wellbeing
I am ready, I am ready, I am ready, I am ready
I am ready for all good things to flow to me easily
I am ready for excitement and eagerness
I am ready for new experiences, places to see, people to meet, things to do
I am ready for a loving relationship that is perfect for me in every way
I am ready for prosperity and abundance beyond measure
I am ready for the joy of feeling sand between my toes
I am ready to feel warmth of the sun warming my back
I am ready to feel the breeze in my face
I am ready for freedom and growth and joy
Thank you Dear God for this wonderful feeling of readiness
I am ready to receive your love and the wonderful things you have lined up for me
I love you. I love life.
I am ready for the guidance that leads me towards improving the abundance that flows to me
Wouldn't it be nice if I could have more money flowing to me
Wouldn't it be nice if things changed in my life for the better in surprising ways
Wouldn't it be nice if new opportunities came to me
I am ready to leave the door of possibility open Dear God
I know it is possible for things to change
I have seen many people improve their situation very quickly
And I want to be like them
I am ready and willing Dear God, I am willing to go where you lead me and do what you lead me to
I am ready to give up all my past believes that no longer serve me and embrace new beliefs that do
I am ready, I am ready, I am ready… and now let the money flow in

100 Prayers

for ultimate joy & success

> Ask and it will be given to you; seek and you will find; knock and the door will be opened to you.
> For everyone who asks receives; the one who seeks finds; and to the one who knocks, the door will be opened.
>
> ~Jesus Christ~

List of prayers

1. Love 41
2. Soar! 44
3. Best 47
4. Enthusiasm 50
5. Benefit 53
6. Unconditional 56
7. Pure 59
8. Spectacular! 62
9. Choose 65
10. Grateful 69
11. Wellbeing 72
12. Rich 75
13. Create 78
14. Sweet 81
15. Harmony 84
16. Special 87
17. Opportunity 90
18. Warmth 94
19. Timing 97

20. Smile 101
21. Strength 104
22. Thrill 107
23. Like 110
24. Better 113
25. Certain 117
26. Receive 120
27. Light 123
28. Gift 125
29. Value 129
30. Believe 132
31. Desire 135
32. Pleasure 138
33. Intention 141
34. Worthy 144
35. Know 147
36. Wisdom 150
37. Marvel 153
38. Willing 156
39. Vibration 159
40. Wish 162
41. Variety 165
42. Good 168

43.	Yes!	171
44.	Thrive	174
45.	Power	177
46.	Passion	180
47.	Celebrate!	184
48.	Amazing	187
49.	Love	191
50.	Potential	195
51.	Anticipation	199
52.	Excited!	202
53.	Accomplish	206
54.	Water	209
55.	Fun!	212
56.	Freedom	215
57.	Nice	219
58.	Thankful	222
59.	Easy	225
60.	Dream	229
61.	New	232
62.	Perfect	235
63.	Discover	238
64.	More	241
65.	Alright	244
66.	Magic	247

67.	Ready	250
68.	Wonder	253
69.	Possibility	256
70.	Impact	259
71.	Beauty	262
72.	Appreciation	265
73.	Inspiration	268
74.	Fantastic!	271
75.	Playful	274
76.	Allowing	277
77.	Energy	280
78.	Unlimited	283
79.	Embrace	286
80.	Shine	289
81.	Happy!	292
82.	Contentment	295
83.	Abundance	298
84.	Knowing	301
85.	Incredible	303
86.	Agree	306
87.	Fun!	309
88.	Trees	312
89.	Praise	315
90.	Satisfaction	318

91.	Clarity	321
92.	Trust	324
93.	Beauty	327
94.	Guidance	330
95.	Joy	332
96.	Decision	335
97.	Align	338
98.	Blessings	340
99.	Relish	343
100.	Vortex	346

Abraham's morning intention 349
About the author 350

Word of the day

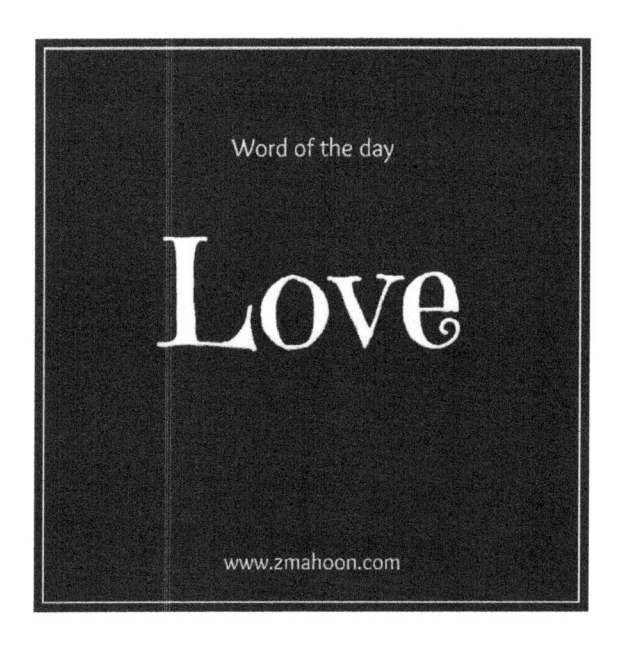

Love

www.zmahoon.com

1. **Love**

Dear God, Thank you for this beautiful new day
I love the feeling of waking up feeling refreshed and happy
I love knowing that all is well in my world
I love the feeling of flowing love

When I flow love it feels like I have sunshine within me
When I flow love it feels like everything and everyone flows love right back at me
When I flow love my day goes really well
When I flow love my children respond to me with love
When I flow love I feel my wellbeing and I know I radiate peace around me
When I flow love I feel easy about everything
When I flow love I know that things are always working out for me

Thank you for the love in my heart
Thank you for the contrast that has helped me learn that love is my anchor
Love is the anchor that keeps me tied to hope
Love is the anchor that keeps me from floating away from those I love
Love is the anchor that keeps me grounded in trust and faith

I love giving love and receiving love, and I want more of that
I want to find things to love about in everyone in my life
I want to be one who is uplifting at all times
I want to be unconditional in the way I live life
I want to make all my decisions from a place of love
I want to act always from a place of love
I love feeling the love you feel for me Dear God
When I feel your love, I know that I am complete
When I feel your love, I feel my own power

When I feel your love, I know that I am unlimited and I can have be or do anything I want
When I feel your love, I feel as if the whole world was made just for me

I want to love myself the way you love me
I want to love the perfection of my being
I want to love the perfection of all others around me
I want to love all of nature
I want to vibrate love and add to the wellbeing of the planet
I am the happiest when I love
I am love

Thank you Dear God for all the love your send my way each day
I love and appreciate all my blessings
I love and appreciate the food I eat
I love and appreciate the things I see
I love and appreciate the songs I hear
I love and appreciate my physical wellbeing
I love and appreciate the prosperity that flows to me
I love and appreciate who I am and who I am becoming
I love and appreciate all those who co-create with me
I love and appreciate my family and friends
I love and appreciate where I live
I love and appreciate the joy that fills my days
I love and appreciate the loving relationships that surround me
Most of all I love and appreciate Your love for me
I love you Dear God. I love me. I love life.

Word of the day

Soar!

www.zmahoon.com

2. Soar!

Dear God, thank you for this brand new day
Today I want to soar to new heights
I love the feeling of elation, when I am elated I feel like I am soaring towards the sky

I love the feeling of a new idea that makes me soar high
It feels like a bird taking flight
It feels like rocket moving at full speed towards the moon
It feels like the power of speed
It feels like clear vision
It feels like control
It feels like ease
It feels unlimited
It feels like an explosion of pure joy
I love that feeling and I can feel it right now in this moment
I love that I can create that feeling inside me just by thinking about it
I love knowing that when I focus on soaring, I am creating events that will give me that feeling

I understand now that my work is to focus on how I want to feel and let You decide what people, things and events will bring me that feeling
I understand that thoughts create and feelings manifest
My heart soars with this knowing
I get it now, I get what my work is
Thank you for this knowing
With this knowing I can soar each day
It is easy to soar towards success
All I have to do is to feel the feeling of success
The feeling of soaring is the feeling of success

The feeling of rising above and beyond
The feeling of touching the sky
The feeling of reaching for more
The feeling of energy travelling at great speed
The feeling of love and joy
The feeling of freedom
When I soar, I feel free – I feel that anything is possible

I love the feeling of all things being possible
I want to wake up each morning and soar like the birds
I want to soar for no reason
I want to soar because I can
I want to soar because it feels good to soar
I want to soar because it is such a good way to start the day
Start the day with a feeling of elation and success pulsing inside me
I can feel a big smile on my face
I can feel my readiness for this beautiful day
I can feel myself radiating with the joy of living
I can feel that I am ready to soar
Bring it on world – I am so ready for you today
I am ready to soar!

Thank you God for this wonderful feeling of power and freedom and joy.
I love you. I love life.

Word of the day

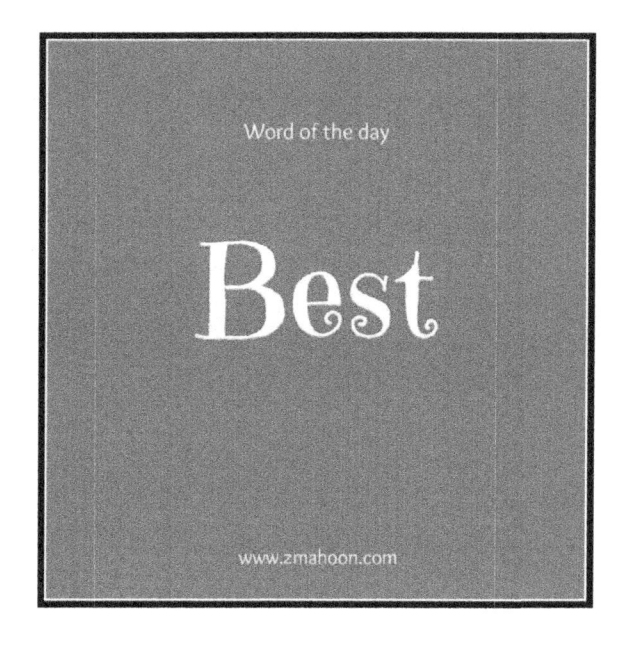

Best

www.zmahoon.com

3. Best

Dear God, thank you for this beautiful new day
A day to be my best

Today I want to focus on being the best version of myself
possible just for now
Today I want to make the best of each moment
Today I want to extract as much joy as I can out of this day

I want to enjoy the sights and sounds of this world
I want to enjoy the food I eat and places I go to and the people I meet
I want to focus on the best that everything has to offer to me
I want to be one who focuses on looking for the best in all people
and all things

When I meet people today I want to look for and find their best qualities
I want good things to come about from my interactions
I want to add value to everyone I come across
I am open to receiving guidance that helps me to offer my best
When I look out on nature I want to look for and find beauty that
makes my heart sing

I want to see the sunshine at it most cheerful, happy best
I want to see the trees waking up and blossoming against the blue sky
I want to see the stars shine at their best
I want to breathe in fresh nourishing air
I want to enjoy the beautiful colours of flowers, birds, and butterflies
I want to appreciate, appreciate, appreciate

When I appreciate I draw out the best in me

When I appreciate I draw out the best in others
When I appreciate I bring the best things in life to me
When I appreciate things go well for me

Appreciation is just a way of looking at things and finding
their best qualities
I can do that – I can appreciate
Today I want to appreciate first then act
I want to appreciate first then talk
I want to appreciate before I do anything
I know that when I appreciate, life gives me more to appreciate
I want that, I like that
I want more things to be happy and appreciative about
Thank you Dear God for helping me be my best
Please keep sending me guidance all day
Please keep reminding me that my work is to look for
and find the best in everything
I love you. I love life.

Word of the day

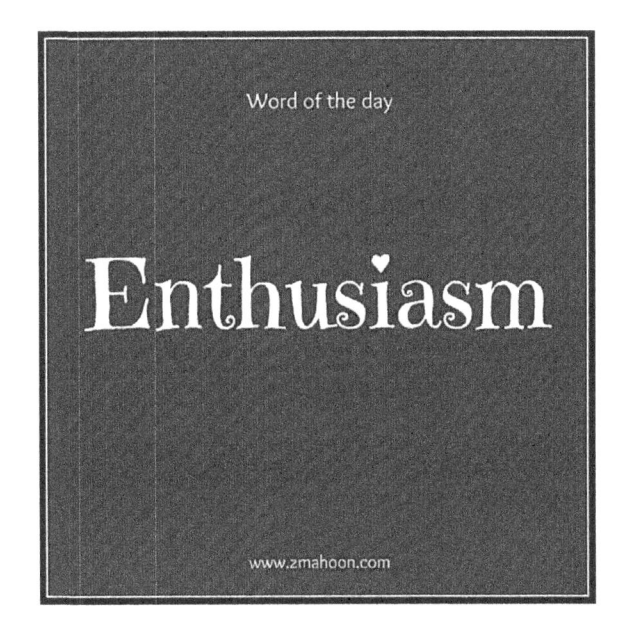

Enthusiasm

www.zmahoon.com

4. Enthusiasm

Dear God, Thank you for this wonderful day
I feel enthusiastic about life today
I know that in every moment I can choose enthusiasm
I know that the attitude from which I think my thoughts has an impact on what happens in my life
I know that when I am enthusiastic, I find more things to be happy and enthusiastic about
And that is what I want Dear God, I want to be happy where I am and enthusiastic for more

Enthusiasm feels like energy moving at great speed
Enthusiasm feels like excitement
Enthusiasm feels like pure joy
I can feel enthusiasm at any time I want to
I can connect with times in the past when I have felt that way
Like the day before going on a long awaited trip
Like waking up on my birthday
Like getting ready to cook a special meal
Like starting a new project
Like meeting up with friends I haven't seen for a while
Like knowing that I've nailed it even before I start
I love feeling the feeling of enthusiasm – it makes me feel alive
That's what enthusiasm is
It is appreciation for what is coming
It is knowing what is coming and feeling excited about it
It's about anticipating fun before it happens
It's about knowing that it's done and letting it in

When I'm enthusiastic I can feel each cell in my body pulsating with energy

When I'm enthusiastic all things feel easy
When I'm enthusiastic life feels good
When I'm, enthusiastic I love people
When I'm enthusiastic people love me
When I'm enthusiastic I have fun and I am fun to be with
When I'm enthusiastic I love me and my life
When I'm enthusiastic I feel like I am flying
When I'm enthusiastic time has no meaning

I love the feeling of enthusiasm
I want more reasons to feel enthusiasm
I know that I must allow myself to feel enthusiastic now,
today, in this moment
And then things and people and events that match that feeling
will show up
I think I can do this
I think I can feel enthusiasm in this moment
I love how rampages of appreciation help me to connect with the feeling of enthusiasm
Thank you for showing me how to do that Dear God
I think I'm ready now
I think I'm ready to bring enthusiasm into my life
I think I'm ready, I think I can feel it
I think I can feel it in this moment
I think I am ready to meet this day with enthusiasm!

Word of the day

Benefit

www.zmahoori.com

5. Benefit

Dear God, Thank you for this wonderful new day
A day to benefit from all the things I've learnt and all the gifts I've received in life
A day to benefit from the guidance that is always there for me
A day to benefit from all the things that are working out for me

I acknowledge that I benefit from so many things every day
I benefit from the air that I breathe in freely, that nourishes me and makes me feel alive
I benefit from the beautiful things I see that make me happy
I benefit from knowing where things are and where I am going because I can see
I benefit from eating good food that provides me with sustenance as well as enjoyment
I benefit from living in a city that I love, in a house that is comfortable and full of warmth
I benefit from the work that I do and the enjoyment that I derive from it, and the money that flows to me because of it
I benefit from the love that surrounds me, that makes me feel blessed everyday
I benefit from the internet and all wonderful places I can go to in the blink of an eye

I benefit from my co-creators in so many ways
I benefit from the doctors and the nurses who look after my loved ones when they need care
I benefit from the mechanics and service people who look after my car and keep it running
I benefit from the people who deliver my mail and collect my trash

I benefit from the engineers who build the roads and the highways and run the transport that I use to get around
I benefit from the trucks and their drivers who bring food from many different places to my grocery store
I benefit from the people who stock shelves and man the cash so that I can get the things I want

I benefit from the teachers who teach my children many wonderful things
I benefit from the friends who include me in their circle of love
I benefit from the guidance that is always leading me towards my wellbeing
I benefit from the support and the assistance from non-physical that is helping me everyday
I benefit from the ideas that pop into my head that make me feel inspired
I benefit from the events that help me to grow and enjoy life to the max
I benefit from God's love, and the many blessings I receive everyday
I benefit from countless things from the time I wake up to when I go to bed
Today I want to consciously appreciate all the things I benefit from
I want to be conscious of the things and people and events that help make my life better
I want to send them all my love and my deepest appreciation, for we are all in this together
Thank you Dear God for the realization that I have much to be grateful for. I love you. I love life.

Word of the day

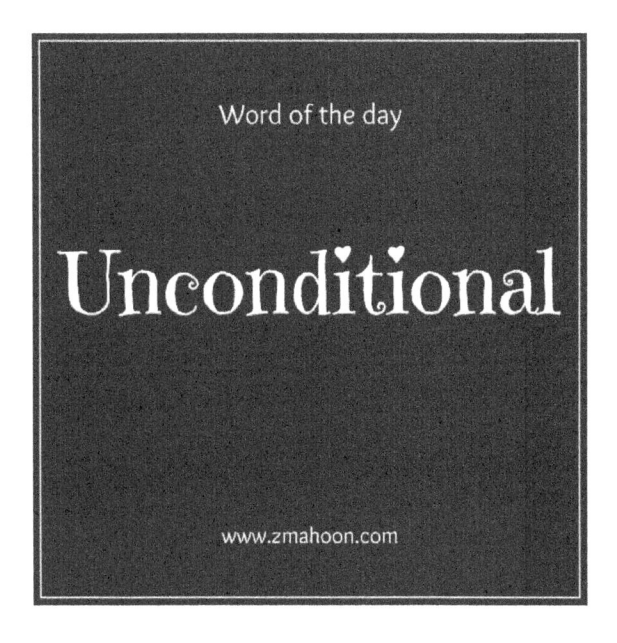

Unconditional

www.zmahoon.com

6. Unconditional

Dear God, Thank you for a wonderful new day, a day to
practice being unconditional
I'm learning that the true path to freedom is through being
Unconditional

Being unconditional means controlling my emotional state
Being unconditional means not waiting for conditions to change in order to feel good
Being unconditional means always responding from a place of love and joy
Being unconditional means emotional stability
Being unconditional means being at peace with the world and its people
I want that
I want to feel in control of my life
I want to feel good
Being emotionally stable feels good

I feel good when I respond from a place of love and joy
I feel good when I have peace within regardless of people and events
I am understanding that being unconditional is not just about my relationship with people
It also has to do with places, things and events
I can express my preferences about the way I like things without pushing against and wanting things to change, and that is the essence of being unconditional
Being unconditional means focusing on something to appreciate
It's about finding a better feeling thought

I can choose to feel unconditional love for divers on the highway weaving in and out of lanes, because I understand that they have to be in alignment to do so

I can choose to feel unconditional love for the slow drivers by appreciating the relaxation they must be feeling rather than focus on their speed

I can choose to feel unconditional love for the neighbours who play loud music when I am trying to sleep because I can focus on the fun they are having and appreciate that

I can choose to feel unconditional love for the electric company and appreciate the energy that makes my house function rather than focus on the bills I have to pay

I can choose to feel unconditional love for my government by focusing on the work they are doing rather than focusing on what remains to be done

I can choose to feel unconditional love for my employers by focusing on the money that flows into my bank account rather than focusing on things I want them to improve

When I focus on an aspect with appreciation, the aspect that I want to improve, improves
I like knowing that
I like knowing that my work is just to find something in everything to appreciate and I know I can do that
I can always find something that feels good so I can always be unconditional
Thank you God for helping me learn how to practice unconditional love, I love you, I love life, I love being unconditional

Word of the day

Pure

www.zmahoon.com

7. Pure

Dear God, Thank you for this beautiful day
I love waking up to a blanket of pure white outside my window
The world looks so beautiful clothed in snow
It looks so untouched, so pure, so lovely
Sunshine and snowfall on the ground are the perfect combination
They fill my heart with pure joy
I love holding my warm mug of coffee and looking out on to the landscape
It is a wonderful way to start my day

Today is going to be a wonderful day
Today I feel pure love for this beautiful world we live in
There is so much beauty for us to feast our eyes on
There is so much life giving energy in the sunshine, it makes me feel so alive
I love the cold crisp air outside and the contrast with the warmth indoors
It feels good to feel the change from winter to spring
I love the feeling of pure joy as I gaze at the budding leaves and flowers
I love the feeling of pure joy as I look at the trees waking up, and I can see how much they have grown
I love the feeling of pure joy as I remember that I too have grown
I have found more freedom, more love for others, more love for me, and a better understanding of how things work

I so appreciate my growth and my journey
I so appreciate all the co-creators who have been and are a part of my journey, I feel pure love for them all
I love the feeling of pure joy in my heart
I can feel that feeling whenever I want to and I know that it is feeling that joy that brings me more things to be happy about

I feel that joy when I hear children laughing and playing in the sun
I feel that joy when I see their smiling happy faces in the morning on their way to school
I feel that joy when I see them laugh for no reason, skip when they could walk, and jump because they can
Children remind me what pure joy looks like and feels like
I want to look for and find that pure feeling of joy in every day
I want to look for and find that pure feeling of joy today!
I know that it is about being light hearted
I know that it is about allowing myself to find things to be joyful and appreciative about
I am learning that joy is my natural state, and I am ready Oh so ready to return to it

Today I want to connect with the feeling of pure joy
Today I want to reach for joy consciously
I want to choose a perspective of joy deliberately
I know I am getting better at this
And I know it is only a matter of time when I will master this completely, and I so looking forward to it

Thank you God for helping me and guiding me at every turn. Thank you for helping me know what pure joy feels like. Thank you for helping me learn that I can create joy simply by wanting it and focusing on it. I love You. I love life. I love joy.

Word of the day

Spectacular

www.zmahoon.com

8. Spectacular!

Dear God, Thank you for another spectacular day
I feel happy today
I feel on top of the world
I feel unlimited possibilities
I see a spectacular future
Life feels good
I love feeling this way

I love feeling energy moving through me
I love the feeling of control that gives me
I love feeling my own power and passion
I love feeling the "all –is-wellness" of things
I love knowing that things are always working out for me
I love knowing that I live in a spectacular world
I love knowing that I have access to spectacular things
I love knowing that there is something pretty spectacular about me
I love knowing that I can always find qualities in other people that surprise and delight me
I love knowing that I can always find spectacular places to visit
I love knowing that there are unlimited spectacular experiences to be had
I love knowing that there is always more to want
I love knowing that there is a deliciousness in wanting
Birthing new desires is more delicious than manifesting them

Life is all about birthing of desire
I am good at that
I have birthed many desires
I love knowing that I don't have to attach myself to any of them

I love knowing that the Universe will always bring me things that I am ready for
I love knowing that life is really simple
I love knowing that simplicity contains spectacular joy
I love knowing that the way I look at things makes them spectacular or not
I love knowing that I can always have a good day
I love knowing that having a good day is a choice
I love knowing that the world is spectacular because I say that it is
I love knowing that I am spectacular because I think I am
I love knowing that my opinion is the only important one
I love knowing that I have a magic wand that can transform any experience, any place, thing or person
And make it spectacular beyond belief – yes! I have that power
And I choose to use it today and everyday

I choose to have a spectacular life
I choose spectacular companions
I choose spectacular experiences
Thank you God for all things spectacular, I love you, I love life.

Word of the day

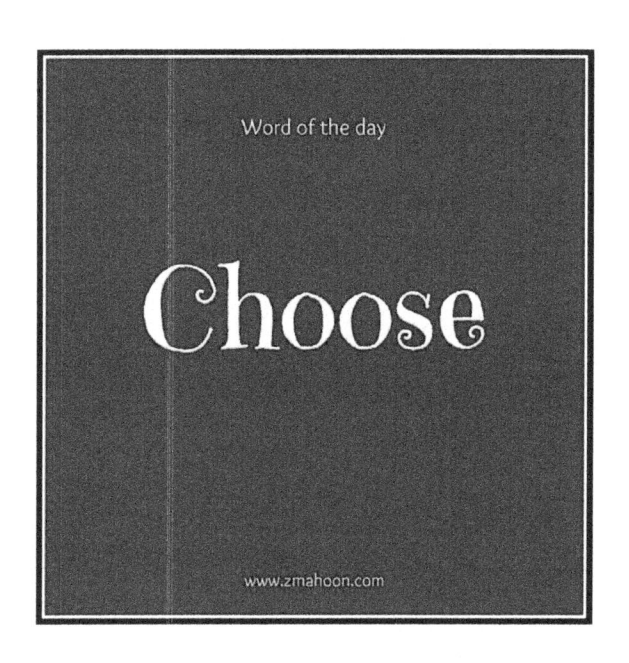

Choose

www.zmahoon.com

9. Choose

Dear God, Thank you for this fantastic new day
A day when I can choose how I want to feel, and what I should think to help me get there
I am thrilled to have the understanding that my work is to choose how I want to feel
And then find a thought that will help me get closer to that feeling place
Today I choose to feel happy
I know that a feeling of joy and happiness means everything is working out for me
And that is what I want, I want things to work out for me in every aspect of my life
And I am willing to pay the price of feeling happy so that things that make me happy can come
I've figured out that when I know how I want to feel then I can think thoughts that help me feel that way, and then doors open, opportunities flow, and miraculous things happen
Today I choose to feel happy
I choose to think about how my heart lifts when I see clear blue skies against the back drop of water and trees
I choose to think about warm sand between my toes, the breeze in my face and the sun warming my back
I choose to appreciate the magnificence of this world
The tall mountains and the rivers that flow
I choose to appreciate the sights and vistas that make my heart sing
I choose to think of how good it feels when my children come and snuggle with me in bed
I choose to think about the cute and funny things they did when they were little that made me laugh

I choose to think about how proud I felt on all their achievements and milestones
I choose to think about the love and joy that fills our lives and our home
I choose to think about how fortunate I am to have the opportunity to do the work I do
I choose to think about how good it feels when I have money flow into my bank account
I know that when I appreciate even the smallest amount of money that comes, like the dime I pick-up from the side walk, more money flows
I know that it's not about how much come, but about the fact that it comes, because I understand that it is as easy to create a castle as it is to create a button
When I get enough practice creating the buttons, the castle will automatically appear
But as long as I keep looking for the castle to appear, I push it away
I choose to appreciate the buttons today, and I choose to create more and more buttons
I choose to think about how many things in my body are working really really well
I choose to appreciate my eyes for helping me see far and wide
I choose to appreciate my legs for carrying me where I want to go
I choose to appreciate my hands for helping me do the work I want to do
I choose to appreciate everything in my body that is working silently without my conscious involvement
I choose to appreciate my life, and where I am
I choose to appreciate that each morning I have the opportunity to shift my focus and therefore change what happens next
I choose to appreciate myself for being willing to learn
I choose to appreciate myself for being one who is dedicated to the feeling of love, joy and freedom

I choose to appreciate myself for being one who is dedicated to the practice of unconditional love

I choose to appreciate myself for my dedication to myself and my life

I choose to appreciate and applaude myself for everything I have done before

I choose to appreciate myself for the work I am doing just now in this moment by looking for things to appreciate

I choose to appreciate all those who are on this journey with me, and all those who are trying to figure it out

I choose to send my love to everyone and everything and to you Dear God

I choose to believe that I have guidance at every step that comes from You

I choose to believe that You are always there helping me, guiding me, supporting me, loving me

I choose to believe that that is all I need in order to continue my journey through life

I love you God, I love my life, I love me, I love all of creation and for now I am complete.

Word of the day

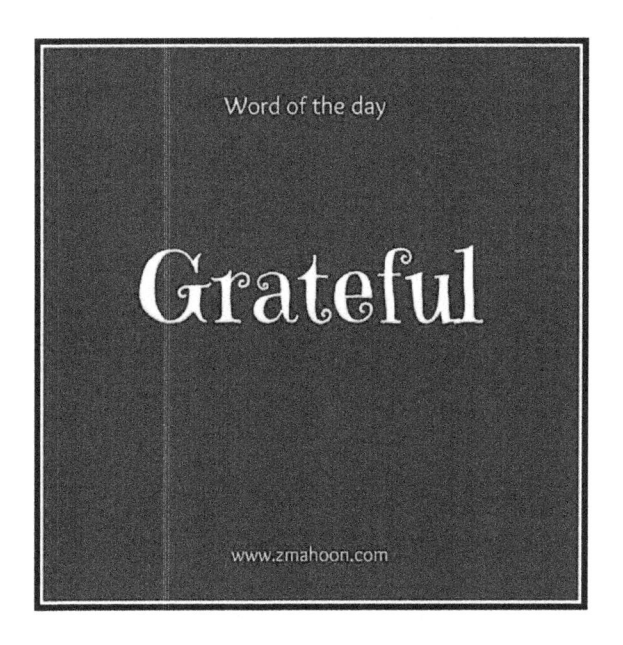

Grateful

www.zmahoon.com

10. Grateful

Dear God, Thank you for a wonderful new day
My heart is overflowing with gratefulness for all the wonderful things in my life
When I look back I am grateful for all the times things have turned out better than I ever expected them to
I am grateful for all the opportunities that came my way and the wonderful people who made my journey easy and fun
I am grateful for my loving parents and I appreciate so much their intention to always do what they thought was best for me
I am grateful for those co-creators who instigated me into understanding and growth
I am grateful for all the events that took place in my life that contributed to who I am today
I am grateful for what I know today, the tools I have picked up that allow me to think my thoughts on purpose
I am grateful because I know how things work and I feel in control of my life experience
I am grateful because I have made the choice to be grateful, because I know that it is the key to a happy life
I am grateful for my beautiful children and the love we share
I am grateful for the work I do and the satisfaction I derive from it
I am grateful for the abundance that flows into my life in so many ways
I am grateful for a good nights' sleep and a comfortable bed
I am grateful for a warm and cozy home, and a hot cup of tea
I am grateful for good friends and loving hearts
I am grateful for the creativity of the people who have created things that make my life easy, like my phone and my computer and the internet, and my car

I am grateful for things like TV and radio and little things like cello wrap and tissue paper
I am grateful for electricity and all the things it runs in my home
I am grateful for warm water to bathe in and wash with
I am grateful for my tooth brush and tooth paste and mouth wash
I am grateful to the person who designed my curtains and my cushions and all the beautiful things in my home
I am grateful for the people who work in the stores where I love to shop
I am grateful for the people who stock the shelves and drive the trucks so that I can get the food I want
I am grateful for the cheerful voice that takes my order at the drive through, and the person at the window who is full of ready humor
I am grateful for the people who clear the snow and keep the highways open
I am grateful for the people who take my garbage away
I am grateful to the scores of volunteers who help in the community, their action helps, but the love they spread goes further than that
I am grateful for those who create entertaining programs for me to watch, and the talented people who act in them, the people who design the costumes and the sets
We are all in this together, we all help each other, we help make the world a beautiful place
There is so much to be grateful for each day
I could sit and write all day about all the things I give thanks for
Thank you God for all these wonderful things
I am learning that joy is about finding little everyday things to be grateful for
I am so grateful Dear God, my heart glows with all the love I am feeling for all the wonderful people who live in this world and all the wonderful things that are part of my life.
I send my love to all and for now I am complete.

Word of the day

Wellbeing

www.zmahoon.com

11. Wellbeing

Dear God, Thank you for a brand new day
I love waking up to a feeling of wellbeing
I love feeling relaxed and happy
I love knowing that a wonderful, happy day lies ahead of me
I love knowing that I can make the conscious decision to enjoy every moment of my day
I love knowing that wellbeing abounds
I love knowing that the natural state of all beings is a state of wellbeing
I love knowing that wellbeing means a feeling of satisfaction, a feeling of joy, a feeling of wellness
I love knowing that I have guidance that tells me the direction of my wellbeing
I love knowing that when I get sideways of my wellbeing I can feel it
I love knowing that my wellbeing is always calling me
I love knowing that all I have to do is to appreciate where I am in order to feel my wellbeing
I love knowing that when I appreciate where I am I allow my wellbeing to flow

I love how I feel when I appreciate
There are so many things for me to appreciate
I feel my wellbeing in the movement of my physical body
I feel my wellbeing when I enjoy good music
I feel my wellbeing when I taste good food
I feel my wellbeing when I breathe in fresh air
I feel my wellbeing when I feel the breeze blowing in my face
I feel my wellbeing when I feel the sun warm my back
I feel my wellbeing when I feel water running over my body
I feel my wellbeing when I laugh and have fun

I feel my wellbeing when I relax and put my feet up
I feel my wellbeing when my children give me warm hugs
I feel my wellbeing when I feel the ease and flow of money in my life
I feel my wellbeing in so many wonderful ways
It's a reminder that more things are working well in my life than not
In fact, things are always working out for me

I love knowing that when I give more attention to what is working my life improves
I love knowing that it is easy to find a place of wellbeing
I love knowing that the stream of wellbeing is always flowing to me
I love knowing that my work is to allow it to flow

I think I am getting better and better at allowing my wellbeing
I think I am becoming more and more conscious about how I pick my thoughts
I think I am learning to tell the difference between positive thoughts and negative thoughts
I think I am ready to put everything I have learnt into practice
I think I am ready to start living life from a place of wellbeing
I think I am ready to start following my guidance towards greater wellbeing
I think I am finally beginning to get it

And I am excited about all the different ways in which it will flow
I am excited about the surprises it will bring
I am eager and hopeful and happy
And I feel powerful, I feel in control of my life experience
This is exciting. Life is exciting. I love my life
I love where I am and I have joyful expectation about what is next.
Thank you God for showing me the way to my wellbeing. I love you. I love life. I love the feeling of wellbeing.

Word of the day

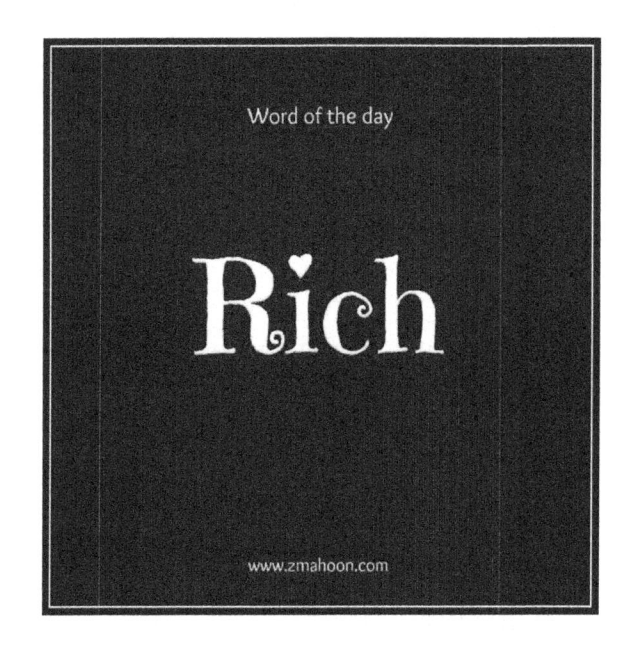

Rich

www.zmahoon.com

12. Rich

Dear God, Thank you for this beautiful day
I love waking up feeling my wellbeing surround me
When I feel my wellbeing I feel rich
When I feel rich I feel prosperous
When I feel rich I feel the ease and flow of life
When I feel rich I feel the abundance of good things in my life

I understand that I am always thinking and therefore I am always creating
I understand that what I think about is what I create
I understand that when I think about the having of something then I create situations that bring the having of it to me
I understand that when I think about the absence of something then I create situations that bring the absence of it to me
I understand now that feeling rich is a matter of perspective
It is a decision I can make every time I think a thought
I can make the decision to appreciate what I have and feel good
Or I can make the decision to notice what is missing and feel bad
I understand that that difference in perspective is the difference between positive thinking and positive creating and negative thinking and negative creating

Today I want to think thoughts that feel good because I want to create good things for myself
Today I want to feel rich and create a future full of riches
When I connect with the feeling of feeling rich in my now, then I create a future that reflects my feeling
I want to create a future that feels good
I want to feel rich in many ways
I can feel rich in many way right now, in this moment

I feel rich in so many wonderful ways
I feel rich when I think about how many friends I have
I feel rich when I think about how blessed I am with my children
I feel rich when I think about my family and loved ones
I feel rich when I think about the love that surrounds me all the time
I feel rich when I sit down to enjoy a wonderful meal
I feel rich when I feel the joy that fills my home
I feel rich when I buy something and bring it home
I feel rich when I am able to keep all my commitments
I feel rich when money comes into my bank account
I feel rich when I think about all the wonderful places I have been to and the wonderful things I have seen

I feel rich when I appreciate the wonderful country where I live
I feel rich when I appreciate nature
I feel rich when I appreciate the abundance of good food
I feel rich when I appreciate the abundance of trees and water
I feel rich when I appreciate the abundance of flowers and plants and animal
I feel rich when I appreciate the beautiful blue sky and the expanse of water in the lakes and the seas
I feel rich when in so many wonderful ways
I love feeling rich
I want more things and people and events in my life that show me how rich I truly am
I am rich in so many ways already and I getting richer in many more ways every day
Thank you Dear God for all the riches in my life. I love you. I love my life.

Word of the day

Create

www.zmahoon.com

13. Create

Dear God, Thank you for a beautiful new day
I am waking up with the realization that I create my own reality
Today I want to create joy, freedom and growth
I want to create love, beauty and pleasure
I am realizing that the art of creating is about feeling the feeling I want to live
And allowing the universe to bring me things, people and events who match the way I feel

I understand now that my work is to manage my feelings
When I feel good, I create and bring to me things, people and events that make me feel good
When I feel unhappy, I create and bring to me things, people and events that make me unhappy
I have decided that I will no longer be passive about creating my reality

I want to create a reality that is full of love, so I must feel full of love today, and then the love that I want will come
I want to create a reality that is full of joy, so I must find a way to feel joy today, and then joyful things will happen
I want to create a reality that is overflowing with prosperity, so I must feel a feeling of abundance today
I want to create a body and a lifestyle that is healthy, so I must feel my health tso oday
I want to create a life that feels of value, so I must feel my value today
I want to create a personality that is confident, so I must feel confident today
I want to create success, so I must feel successful today
That's the key and I have it

I can find things to focus on that help me to feel the feeling that I want to feel
I can be conscious of the way I am feeling in any moment and change it so that I can control the reality that I create

Creation is all about emotion, and thought is the tool that I can use to generate the emotion and then all the things that match my emotions will flow to me easily

I can do this; I can think and feel and create on purpose
I want to be one who lives life powerfully and on purpose
I want to be one who is satisfied at the end of every day
I want to be one who understands creation and uses the law of attraction consciously
I want to be one whose life is magical
I want to be one who is happy
I want to be one who flows unconditional love
I want things to work out for me in many wonderful ways

Thank you God for helping me understand the power of my guidance system and the power of my thought
I love knowing that I have complete control over what I create. I love You. I love life. I love creation.

Word of the day

Sweet

www.zmahoon.com

14. Sweet

Dear God, Thank you so much for this wonderful new day
Another day to extract joy from life
Today I want to feel how sweet my life is
I want to master the art of getting to that sweet spot where life always feels good

I want to learn to live in a constant state of appreciation just like my cat
I love how she is always purring her appreciation of life, she lives in the sweet spot
She appreciates me, she appreciates her food, she appreciates her naps
She teaches me to appreciate
She holds her love for me constant
Even on days when her bowl is empty
Even on days when I forget to brush her
Even on days when she has no fresh water
She is always happy to see me, always showing me her complete appreciation
She only co-creates with me when she is feeling good
She shows me the true meaning of unconditional love
She lives life in the sweet spot

I want to learn to live in a constant state of trust and faith just like the trees
I love how trees always stay rooted in their faith, trusting that everything they need will come to them and it does
Trees never question why winter is so long
They never throw a tantrum when there is no rain
They make the most of the sunshine
They always share their fruit with the world
They always give of themselves because they trust in the abundance of the universe
They live life in the sweet spot
I want to be like the trees firmly rooted and always reaching for light

I love how birds always allow themselves to be guided where to go to find food
They spread their wings and enjoy their physicality

They allow their guidance to shelter them from the weather
They trust that their young ones have guidance too, and they show them how to use it
Then they let them go and find their own way in the world
They live life in the sweet spot
I want to learn how to allow my guidance to lead me at all times
I want to be like the birds, going with the flow without asking why
Birds wake up and sing songs of appreciation
Birds wake up and fly, they allow their guidance to lead them to food and shelter
They allow their guidance to lead them when they migrate
Everything they do is based on guidance
They live life in the sweet spot
That's what I want, I want to allow my guidance to lead me where I need to go, to show me what I need to do
I want to live life in the sweet spot

Appreciation, trust, and allowing my guidance
That's all I need in order to get to the sweet spot
Today I want to offer conscious appreciation of where I am, where I have been and where I am going
Today I want to trust that all is well and things always work out for me
Today I want to allow my guidance to help me with everything I want
Today I want to live life in the sweet spot
Thank you God for showing me that life in the sweet spot is the only thing worth aiming for
Thank you for showing me that it is easy to get to the sweet spot
Today is the perfect day to start living in the sweet spot

Word of the day

Harmony

www.zmahoon.com

15. Harmony

Dear God, Thank you for blessing me with your love
Thank you for the peace and harmony in my heart
Thank you for the ease and flow of my life
Thank you for the love that surrounds me at all times
Thank you for the food we eat
Thank you for the love we share
Thank you for the abundance we have
Thank you for the wellbeing in our lives
Thank you for the harmony we share
Thank you God for everything
I can see how everything in nature is in harmony with each other and with You
There is harmony in the transition between day and night
There is harmony in the transition between summer and winter
There is harmony in the transition between life and death
I understand that going with the flow creates harmony in my life
I understand that when I am in harmony with my emotional guidance I feel good
I understand that when I feel good I am in harmony with that which I consider to be good
I understand that when I feel good I am attracting people, things and events that feel good
I want to feel good
I want to be in harmony with the energy that creates worlds
I want to be in harmony with my wellbeing
I want to be in harmony with my emotional guidance
I want to be in harmony with all of nature
I want to be in harmony with the abundance that is flowing to me at all times

I want to be in harmony with my physical body, allowing it to do it's job
I want to be in harmony with joyful people, and joyful events
I want to be in harmony with loving co-creators
I want to be in harmony with laughter and fun
I want to be in harmony with warm hearts
I want to be in harmony with those who are interested in my work
I want to be in harmony with people who are playful and curious
I want to be in harmony with the trees, standing in appreciation of this world
I want to be in harmony with flowing water, always finding its way
I want to be in harmony with beautiful flowers so that I may see more of those
I want to be in harmony with more opportunities to travel and see the world
I want to be in harmony with the feeling of satisfaction for work well done
I want to be in harmony with the feeling of elation for success that comes with ease
I want to be in harmony with the world and all its beings
I want to be in harmony with all that is good
I want to be in harmony with God and my inner guidance
Today I want to feel the feeling of being in harmony, the feeling of being one with the world
Being in harmony means appreciating where I am and where I want to go
Today I will consciously look for things to appreciate and be happy about
Today I will seek harmony
Today I want to end my day feeling happy with the harmony I have felt all day
The delicious feeling of being in the flow
Thank you God for showing me that it is easy to appreciate and therefore it is easy to be in harmony
And when I am in harmony all good things flow easily into my life
I love feeling the harmony of living. I love You. I love life.

Word of the day

Special

www.zmahoon.com

16. Special

Dear God, Thank you for this very special day
A day to enjoy being alive
A day to appreciate all my blessings
A day to think on purpose and create a joyful future

I feel special when I think about all the wonderful things in my life
I feel special when I think that I have been blessed with the most amazing children
I love and appreciate my children, they give me a reason to flow love
They are special and they make me feel special
I feel special because I have wonderful friends
I feel special because I live in a beautiful place
I feel special because I have abundance flowing to me in so many ways
I have an abundance of people to love who love me
I have an abundance of energy flowing through me
I have an abundance of good health, for there are many things in my body that are working perfectly
I have an abundance of things that make me happy, like the blue sky, and the beautiful trees and the water flowing in the streams
I have an abundance of good food to taste and enjoy
I have an abundance of music to listen to that lifts my spirits and makes me feel good

These are just some of the things that make me feel special
There are so many things that remind me every day how special I am
I feel special when I look up at the sky and feel the presence of God
I feel special knowing that all that love is pointed at me
I feel special knowing that I have guidance that is always calling me towards my wellbeing

I feel special knowing that I can have, be or do anything I want
I feel special knowing that when I ask it is always given
I feel special knowing that I am unlimited
I feel special knowing that I am always connected to the stream of wellbeing that is God
I feel special knowing that I am at the centre of my universe
I feel special knowing that all of nature is there to support me
I feel special knowing that there are non-physical forces assisting me at all times
I feel special knowing that things are always working out for me
I feel special knowing that all is always well
I feel special knowing that my work here is to have fun
I feel special knowing that I am always cared for
I feel special knowing that when I call God is always there listening
I feel special knowing that God is listening even when I'm not calling
I feel special Dear God, I feel special

Thank you for always being there for me, loving me, assisting me, helping me, guiding me, showing me in so many ways that I am of value, that I am worthy, that I am special, that I can have, be or do anything I want
I love you. I love life. I love feeling special.

Word of the day

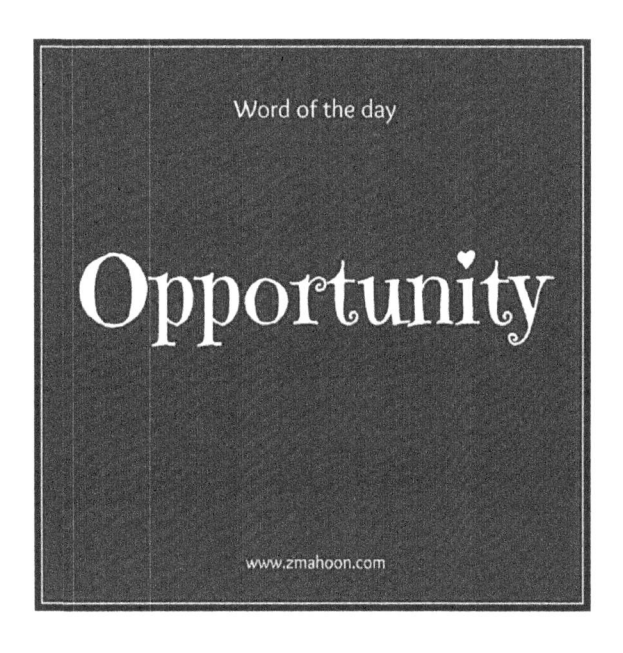

Opportunity

www.zmahoon.com

17. Opportunity

Dear God, Thank you for this beautiful new day
An opportunity to start again

I love knowing that every new day is a new beginning
It is an opportunity to consciously pick my thoughts and feel my emotions
To tune myself to the never ending stream of wellbeing that is always flowing to me
Waking up in the morning is an opportunity for me to choose thoughts of appreciation
It is an opportunity to love again, love myself, love the world I live in and love everyone who co-creates with me

I want to make the most of this opportunity today
I love and appreciate the opportunity to wake up in the morning
I love and appreciate the opportunity to spend another day enjoying my children
I love and appreciate the opportunity to bask in the sunshine
I love and appreciate the opportunity to walk and jump and feel the strength and dexterity of my physical body
I love and appreciate the opportunity to think better feeling thoughts and to consciously create a future with more joy and more freedom
I love and appreciate the opportunity to find things to love and appreciate

I understand that in every moment I have the opportunity to choose how I want to feel and then think those thoughts that will give me that feeling
I understand that when I use this process of thinking my life keeps getting better and better and better
And I keep finding more things to be happy and appreciative about

I love knowing that each day is an opportunity to start fresh
I love knowing that I have the opportunity to set the tone for my day
I love knowing that yesterday doesn't matter and that tomorrow is another opportunity
I love knowing that I can never go wrong and I can never get it done, because life is a continuous journey of opportunities
I love knowing that I am the creator of my opportunities
I love knowing that my thoughts create the doors that my actions will open
I love knowing that I am a conscious creator
I love knowing that I have great power
I love knowing that the Universe responds to my every thought
I love knowing that I have the opportunity to be light hearted today and every day
I love knowing that when I am light hearted I create more fun and more joy in my future
I love knowing that the opportunity to have fun is created by the emotion of feeling fun, I can do that

The opportunity to love is created by the emotion of feeling love, I can do that
The opportunity to be free is created by the emotion of feeling free, I can do that
The opportunity to be prosperous is created by the emotion of feeling abundance, I can do that
The opportunity to be healthy is created by the emotion of feeling wellbeing, I can do that
The opportunity to feel joy is created by the emotion of feeling joy, I can do that
The opportunity to be successful is created by the emotion of feeling success, I can do that

The opportunity to feel excited is created by the emotion of feeling excitement, I can do that
The opportunity to feel satisfied is created by the emotion of feeling satisfaction, I can do that

I can do it, I can do it, I can do it
I can feel the emotion first and then the thing that gives me that emotion is sure to come
I can feel the power of my desires and I can feel the power of my emotions and my thinking process
I can do this Dear God, I can do this, I have the key to everything I want

In this moment I have the opportunity to change my entire life and be the person I want to be and life the life I want to live
Thank you for this amazing opportunity. I love you. I love life. I am ready to create my opportunities.

Word of the day

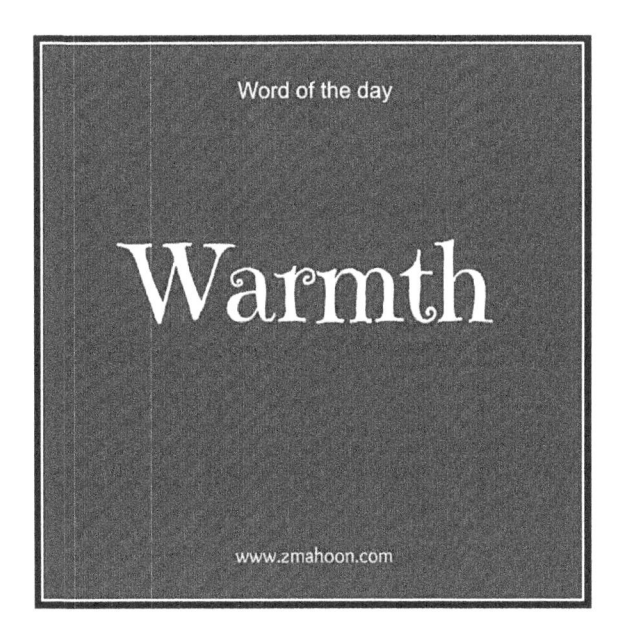

Warmth

www.zmahoon.com

18. Warmth

Dear God, Thank you for this beautiful warm day
I love waking up to golden sunshine streaming into my room
I love looking out of my window to see the sun warming the Earth
I absolutely love the sun warming my back
I love how sunshine brightens the day
I love the feel of walking on the beach with warm sand between my toes
I love the feel of smooth rocks warmed by the sun
I love how wonderful it feels when my cat snuggles with me; I love feeling her warmth against me
I love warm hugs from my children, I love holding them tight
I love the warmth of having them snuggle with me in bed
I love the warmth of meeting old friends and catching up with all their news
I love how warm and cozy it feels to sit by the fireplace sipping my coffee when it's cold outside
I love coming in from the snow and smelling the warm smell of hot chocolate
I love how warm and friendly my home feels

Thank you for all the warmth in my life
I feel the warmth of loving all the beautiful people in my life
I feel the warmth of friendship for all those who play with me
I feel the warmth of caring for nature, plants and animals
I feel the warmth of beautiful smiles, and big hearts
I love feeling my heart warming up to a story about love and caring
I love feeling the warmth rising from my heart and spreading throughout my body

It feels good to love
It feels good to feel the warmth of love surround me

I love the peace that comes with feeling this way
I want more opportunities to feel the warmth of love in my life
I want to give love and receive love
I want to be surrounded by the warmth of good friendship
I want to be warm hearted towards all those whose lives I touch
I want my warmth to make a difference in the world
I want to feel my value
I want to feel my power
I want to feel my warmth
I want to feel worthy
I want to feel happy
I want to feel peace within my heart

Thank you Dear God for helping me understand that a warm heart is a loving heart
Thank you for helping me understand that it is just as important to love myself as it is to love others
Thank you for the warmth of love and guidance that I always feel from you
Thank you for always being with me, helping me, guiding me, calling me towards my wellbeing
I send the warmth of my love around the world to all living beings
I love my life. I love me. I love the feeling of warmth in my heart.

Word of the day

Timing

www.zmahoon.com

19. Timing

Dear God, Thank you for this wonderful new day
I feel happy and refreshed, ready to enjoy my day
I love and appreciate all the blessings in my life
I love and appreciate the beautiful world I live in and the beautiful people I meet
I love and appreciate the food I eat and the clothes I wear and the house I live in
I love and appreciate who I am and who I am becoming

My life is good, and I am beginning to appreciate the perfect timing in everything that happens
I am beginning to understand that the timing of things depends on my ability to line-up
And my ability to line-up depends on my ability to appreciate
Timing is about the momentum of desire relative to the momentum of expectation
The difference between those two is equal to the timing of things in my life
When my desire is huge and my expectation is not, timing stretches out
When my expectation is high, even my smallest desire is manifested right away!

I understand that when the momentum of negative beliefs is higher than the pulling power of my desires, things take longer
I understand that when I question the timing of things I push manifestations away
I understand that I can control my manifestations by controlling my thoughts
When I appreciate where I have been and where I am and where I am going I create positive momentum

Dear God, I am ready today, I am ready to give up all beliefs that no longer serve me
I am ready to embrace beliefs that open me up to unlimited possibilities
I am ready to be one who is in control of my own life experience
I am ready to embrace ways of thinking that bring me more wellbeing
I am ready, I am ready, I am ready
I am ready to believe that anything is possible
I am ready to believe that I have guidance
I am ready to believe that I intuitively know how to use my guidance
I like thinking that my life can just keep getting better and better
I like thinking that I am in control of my life experience
I like thinking that when I'm feeling good, the timing of all things is perfect

I can see evidence in the world that shows me that You always have perfect timing
Everything in nature has perfect timing
Because everything in nature trusts in perfect timing
Because everything in nature allows You to have your way
Because everything in nature is open to all possibilities
The sun always rises with perfect timing
The seasons always change in perfect timing
Birds always migrate in perfect timing
Planets always travel in perfect timing
The tide always comes in perfect timing
Today I declare that I am open to all possibilities

I declare that I want my expectations to match up with my desires
I declare that I want to allow my guidance
I declare that I want wellbeing to prevail
I declare that I want to feel the perfect timing of all things
I declare that I want to think my thoughts on purpose

I declare that I want to be a powerful creator
I declare that I want to feel ease and flow on all subjects
I declare that I want to feel good
I declare that I am ready to do what it takes to feel good
Thank you God for this day to learn more and grow more and be happy. I love You. I love life.

Word of the day

Smile!

www.zmahoon.com

20. Smile

Dear God, Thank you for another wonderful day
Today I am thinking how a smile changes the way people look and feel
I love the smiles that make people look happy
Lips that smile are beautiful
Eyes that smile are energizing
Hearts that smile are captivating
Smiles are a sign of wellbeing
Smiles are a sign of love
Smiles are a sign of joy
Smiles are what we are all reaching for

I smile when I see the sun shining
I smile when I see people having fun
I smile when I have fun
I smile when I see children laughing and playing
I smile when I look out on to trees and beautiful vistas
I smile when I meet friends
I smile when my food tastes good
I can choose to smile at any time
I can choose to smile in response to things
Or I can smile and create things that make me smile
Today I want to be one who smiles
I understand now that I don't need for things to happen that will make me smile
I understand that when I smile, things happen that bring me joy

Smiling is my body's natural response to feeling good
When I feel good I smile
I can tell when others are feeling good because I can see their smiles

I can see the smiles in their eyes and on their faces
And I can feel the smiles in their hearts
Smiling faces are like sunshine, they spread joy
Smiling eyes are like stars, they give hope
Smiling hearts are like warm hugs, they spread love all around
Smiles are amazing because they have the power to change things
A smile can change a mood
A smile can give hope
A smile can convey love
We all love smiles and we all have smiles to give and receive
I love to see children smiling and laughing in the morning on their way to school
I love to see people having fun

Today I want to smile at everyone I meet
I want to smile with my lips
I want to smile with my eyes
I want to smile with my heart
I want to smile because it feels good
I want to smile because it is the easiest thing to do
I want to smile because it makes me happy
I want to see others smile back at me
I want to see the whole world smiling
I want to feel wellbeing all around me and inside me

Smile because it's easy
Smile because it feels good
Smile because I can
Thank you Dear God for giving me so many things to smile about. I love you.
I love my life.

Word of the day

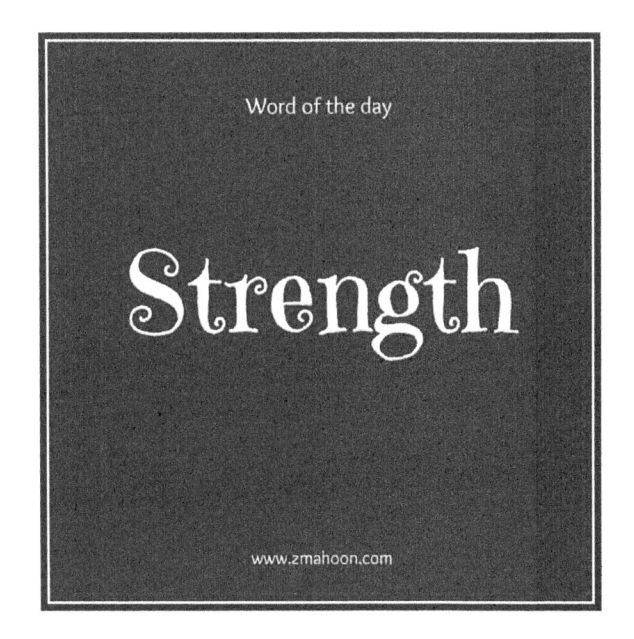

Strength

www.zmahoon.com

21. Strength

Dear God, Thank you for another amazing day
I am realizing some important things today
I am realizing that I have spent a very long time trying to be strong
Whatever came I stood tall and unbending – I held my own
I dug in my heels and refused to go
Today, I am realizing that my strength is in surrendering

When I surrender I go with the flow, I go with my guidance
When I surrender life is easy
When I surrender I relax
When I surrender I become one with the Universe and then I feel strong
Real strength is in surrendering

My strength is in allowing you to guide me towards my wellbeing
My strength is in allowing my guidance by making peace with where I am
My strength is in looking for and finding something to appreciate about everything
My strength is in flowing love
My strength is in being a conscious and deliberate creator
My strength is in thinking thoughts on purpose
My strength is in listening to my emotional guidance
My strength is in hanging on to my faith
My strength is in knowing that things always work out for me
My strength is in knowing that all is always well
My strength is in enjoying every day
My strength is in being easy on myself and on others
My strength is in trusting my guidance system
My strength is in knowing how to think my thoughts
My strength is in teaching from the power of my own experience

What makes me strong is my capacity to love
What makes me strong is my capacity for learning
What makes me strong is my faith in You Dear God

I know what strength feels like
Strength feels like the power of knowing
Strength feels like standing on a mountain top and looking down on the world
Strength feels like feeling energy pulsating through my body
Strength feels like positive expectation
Strength feels like being one with the Universe
Strength feels like knowing that anything is possible
Strength feels like knowing that what I want is possible
Strength feels like knowing that the Universe has my back
When I feel strong I feel invincible
When I feel strong I am one with the Universe
When I feel strong my body reflects it to me
When I feel strong everything seems easy
When I feel strong I have knowing
When I feel strong I love myself and everyone else
When I feel strong I know I am at the right place at the right time

I want to feel strong today
I want to be one with the Universe
Thank you Dear God for helping me realize what true strength
Please guide me towards surrender, and attitude of ease and flow, for that is where my strength is
Whenever I feel like digging in my heels I will let go and let you guide me towards my strength
I love you. I love life. I love my strength.

Word of the day

Thrill

www.zmahoon.com

22. Thrill

Thank you Dear God for another beautiful day
I feel thrilled to be alive today
Thrilled to wake up to beautiful sunshine and a blue blue sky
Thrilled to see how beautiful the world looks outside my window
Thrilled to stretch and feel energy flowing through my body
Thrilled to smell the beautiful aroma of fresh coffee
Thrilled to take that first delicious invigorating sip

I've begun to realize that thrill is a feeling I can decide to have
I have to bring thrill to whatever I gaze on and whatever I do
I have to feel the emotion first and then focus
Life is about creating an emotional net to catch events, relationships and things in
I am learning that when I create the emotion first, then everything that falls into it's net corresponds with the emotion I feel
When I cast the net of joy I catch more joy
When I cast the net of love I catch more love
When I cast the net of satisfaction I catch more satisfaction
All vibrational work is about casting the right emotional net
Today I want to cast a net that is made up of thrill
I can cast that net anytime I want by focusing on events in the past when I felt that way

Like the thrill I feel driving on an open road with the breeze in my face
Like the thrill I felt when I held my babies for the first time
Like the thrill I feel every time I'm on a boat
Like the thrill I feel when I'm in an aircraft that's taking off
Like the thrill I feel when I look at tall mountains and beautiful waterfalls
Like the thrill I feel when I have an aha moment and things fall into place

Like the thrill I feel when a good friend shows up unexpectedly
Like the thrill I feel when I cook and I just know that it's turning out perfect
I can close my eyes and thrill in those moments over and over again every day
And as I do that I cast the net that brings more of such moments to me
I thrill in knowing how the universe works
I thrill in knowing Gods system for granting wishes
I thrill in knowing that the thrill has to come before the event not as a result of the event I want
I thrill in knowing what a long way I've come and how easy my life has become

I want more thrilling moments in my life
I want more joy, I want more abundance
I want more health, I want more satisfaction
Therefore I must find joy so that joy can come
I must find the feeling of abundance so that abundance can come
I must feel healthy so that health can come
I must feel satisfaction so that satisfaction can come
I must feel thrilled so that more thrilling moments can come
It is wonderful that I live in a world where there are so many opportunities for me to look around me and find things to feel happy and thrilled about
Thank you God for the knowledge I have, I am thrilled to know these important things
I am thrilled to be the creator of my life experience. I love you. I love life.
I am thrilled to be alive

Word of the day

Like

www.zmahoon.com

23. Like

Dear God, Thank you for a brilliant beautiful new day
I like waking up and looking at a blue blue sky
I like waking up and feeling refreshed and happy
I like feeling energized for my day
I like the feeling of knowing that all is well, and that things are always working out for me
I like knowing that the contrast of this world serves me, it is my friend
I like knowing that it is through experiencing contrasting things that I am able to define my preferences
I like knowing that all I have to do is to focus on what I like

When I focus on things that I like I vibrate on the frequency of love and appreciation
When I love and appreciate only then can I attract the things that I want
When I love and appreciate it doesn't matter what comes, because I am always able to find something I like about it
It feels good to like and love and enjoy
It feels easier to find things to like and appreciate than not
I can always find something to like about every body
I know when I focus on finding things to like about people; people are nice to me
When I focus on liking people, I have more fun with them
When I focus on liking people, they assist me in my endeavours
When I focus on liking people, they like me!

Today I want to consciously look for something to like and appreciate about everyone I meet
It feels good to think that I can do that
I like knowing that when I send my love to animals, they reflect it back to me

I like saying hello to the black birds and the crows
I like watching them as they bend their heads and look at me as if to acknowledge my greeting
I like telling the dogs I meet on my morning walk how beautiful they are
I like looking into their eyes and knowing that they know
I like appreciating the trees and telling each one that it is perfect
I like sending them my love and I know that they always send love back to me
I like looking into the eyes of a baby and seeing how eager they are for life
I like my cat purring in my ear to wake me up in the morning
I like waking up to a quiet house ad feeling the all is wellness of my world
I like holding my morning coffee in my hands and looking out on to the beauty of a new day
I like finding the perfect parking and knowing that I created it
I like getting a free cart at the grocery store and knowing that I created it
I like finding things on sale that were on my list and knowing that I created it
I like chatting with good friends and knowing that I created that friendship
I like money flowing easily into my life and knowing that I created it
I like feeling the health and stamina of my body and knowing that I created it
I like the relaxation of coming home at the end of the day, knowing that it was a good day
I like the feeling of satisfaction of a day well lived
I like knowing that I am the creator of my life
I like knowing that all the things I desire exist and are on their way to me
I like knowing that all I have to do is to trust in my guidance and allow my natural wellbeing
Thank you Dear God for giving me the opportunity to find so many things to like
I like my life. I like me. I like all of creation.

Word of the day

Better

www.zmahoon.com

24. Better

Thank you Dear God for this wonderful new day
Today I want to think on purpose
Today I want to think thoughts that create ease and flow in my life
I realize that I can always say it better
I know that what I say creates my reality
I know that I can say it better and create a better reality for myself
I rendezvous with the things I think about

I can say it better
I am getting better at rendezvousing with the things I think about
I can say it better
I'm pretty good at rendezvousing with the things I like
I can say it better
No matter what I am rendezvousing with, I like it because it is an indicator of what I am doing vibrationally
I can say it better
I love the contrast that helps me to clarify what I really want
I can say it better
Contrast helps me to clarify what I really want
I can say it better
I love finding out what I really want
I can say it better
I like being the creator of my own reality

I can say it better
I like controlling my thoughts to create a reality I like
I can say it better
I like directing my thoughts in positive ways
I can say it better

I like thinking on purpose
I can say it better
I like thinking thoughts that feel good
I can say it better
I like feeling good
I can say it better
I love feeling good
I can say it better
I feel good quite often
I can say it better

I feel good most of the time
I can say it better
I can feel good whenever I want
I can say it better
The better I feel the better it gets
I can say it better
I feel good when I flow love
I can say it better
I am one who flows love
I can say it better
I am love, therefore I flow love
I can say it better
I love loving and I am good at that
I can say it better
I control my thoughts therefore I control my life
I can say it better
I am good at controlling my thoughts, therefore I am good at controlling my life
I can say it better
I am happy with the life I am living

I can say it better
I am happy where I am and eager for more
I can say it better
I am on my way to better things
I can say it better

Things are always working out for me
I can say it better
I love my life. I love me. I love God.
I can say it better
I am good at creation, I am ready for creation
I can say it better
I am ready for whatever comes
Because I always have guidance and because I have guidance I always know what to do
I am ready, I am ready, I am ready, I am ready
Bring it on world, I am ready
I am ready to have, be and do everything I want

Word of the day

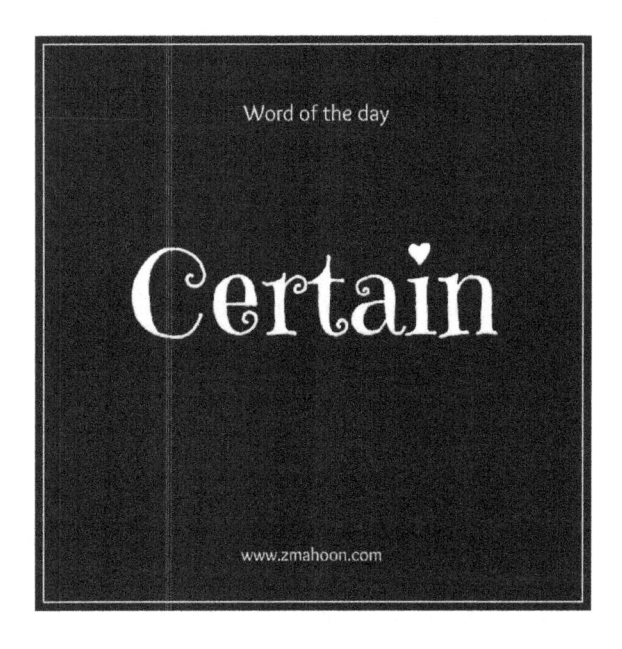

Certain

www.zmahoon.com

25. Certain

Dear God Thank you for this wonderful new day
I love waking up feeling certain that I am happy and relaxed
I love waking up and feeling certain that I will have a good day
I love waking up and feeling certain that I will enjoy my morning coffee
I love the certainty of knowing that the sun will always rise and there will always be a new day

I love the certainty of knowing that spring will always follow winter
I love the certainty of knowing that when a tree dies a new one is born
I love the certainty of knowing that there is perfect balance in the universe
I love the certainty of knowing that the law of attraction is always fair
I love the certainty of knowing that my guidance is always there for me
I love the certainty of knowing that God always loves me
I love the certainty of knowing that things are always working out for me
I love the certainty of knowing that my children love me
I love the certainty of knowing that I love my children unconditionally
I love the certainty of knowing that I am the creator of my life
I love the certainty of knowing that I can have, be or do anything I want
I love the certainty of knowing that all things are possible
I love the certainty of knowing that my prosperity is given
I love the certainty of knowing that I can find joy in every day
I love the certainty of knowing that I can trust my body to respond to me
I love the certainty of knowing that contrast is a good thing
I love the certainty of knowing that my thoughts are powerful
I love the certainty of knowing that I am a powerful being
I love the certainty of knowing that I have a loving heart

I love the feeling of certainty
Today I want to feel certain

I want to feel certain that I can sniff out and follow the path of ease and flow
I want to feel certain that I can control my thoughts and think on purpose
I want to feel certain that all things in the universe respond to me
I want to feel certain of my power and my passion for life
Feeling certain is the feeling of sureness that comes from trust and faith

I am certain that I can trust the guidance that is always there for me
And because I trust my guidance
My wellbeing is certain
My prosperity is certain
My joy is certain
My happiness is certain
My success is certain
My health is certain
My joyous co-creation with others is certain

The manifestation of my every desire is certain
The love of God is certain.
I love you Dear God. I love me. I love life
I can walk through life feeling certain that life is about being joyful
It is about being loving towards myself and others
It is about going with the flow
I love the feeling of certainty about all subjects and I want more of that
Dear God please always guide me towards that which I can feel with certainty is good for me and will bring me joy. Thank you for your love and your guidance. I love you. I love life.

Word of the day

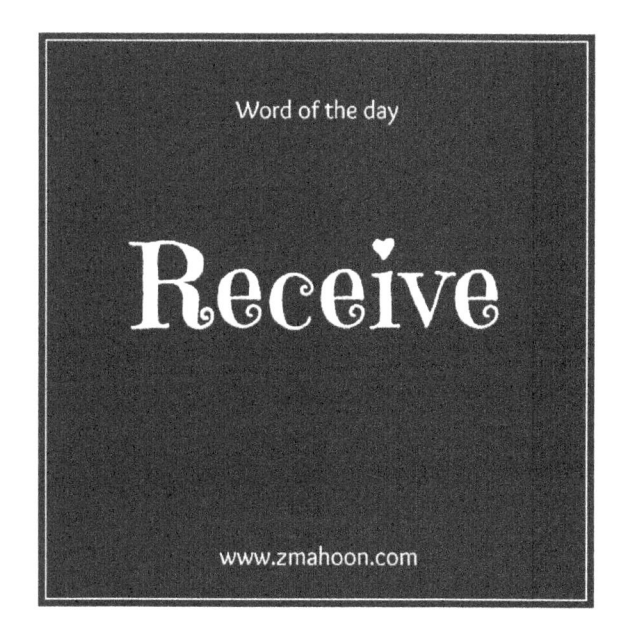

Receive

www.zmahoon.com

26. Receive

Dear God, Thank you for another amazing day
Today I want to live life in the receptive mode
Receiving all the things I want
Thank you for teaching me the value of the receptive mode

I know now that I can only receive when I am in the receptive mode
I know now that it is easy to get to the receptive mode
I know now that all I have to do to get into the receptive mode is to appreciate
I know that the receptive mode is a place of joy
I know that the receptive mode is a place of love
I know that all I have to do is to flow love unconditionally in order to live my life in the receptive mode

I love being in the receptive mode, I love flowing love and feeling joy
It is easy to flow love and feel joy
I can do that in this moment
I can find things to love and appreciate in every moment
I love and appreciate my wellbeing and I want to receive more of that
I love and appreciate the joy I feel as I gaze at my children and I want to receive more of that
I love and appreciate the feeling of abundance I feel when money comes into my bank account and I want to receive more of that
I love and appreciate the feeling of freedom that I feel when the breeze touches my face and I want more of that
I love and appreciate the feeling of power I feel when my physical body responds to what I ask of it and I want more of that
I love and appreciate the delicious tasting foods I eat and I want more of that

I want to be one who lives life in the receptive mode
I want to feel the ease and flow of the receptive mode
I want to feel the unlimited feeling of the receptive mode
I want to live an unconditional way of life in the receptive mode
I want to live a life full of wonder and creativity in the receptive mode

Today and everyday I want to be open to receiving the goodness and the wellbeing that is lined up for me
Today I am open to receiving
Today I am open to receiving wellbeing
Today I am open to receiving love
Today I am open to receiving abundance
Today I am open to receiving joy
Today I am open to receiving all good things
Today I am open to receiving guidance
Today I am open to receiving satisfaction
Today I am open to receiving new experiences
Today I am open to receiving new opportunities
Today my heart is open to trust

As I stand here today Dear God, I am open to receiving
I am open to receiving all that you have lined up for me
I am joyful and content and happy
My heart is open to receiving your love and your guidance
Thank you for helping me find the receptive mode.
I love you. I love life. I love being in the receptive mode.

Word of the day

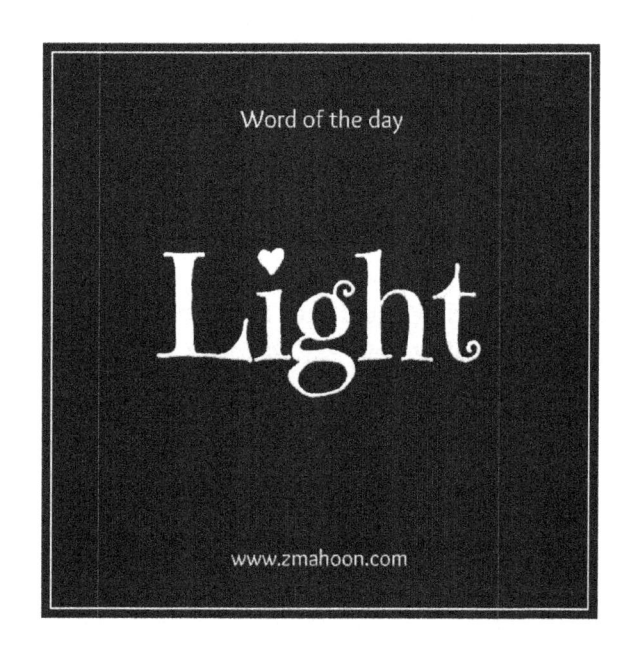

Light

www.zmahoon.com

27. Light

Dear God thank you for shining your light on the world
The day dawns because of your light
The birds sing because of your light
The crops grow because of your light
The fruits ripen because of your light
The waters glisten because of your light
The world wakes up because of your light
The world thrives because of your light

My heart is full of joy because of your light
I know my guidance because of your light
I can see my path because of your light
I can help others because of your light
I am who I am because of your light
All my joys are because of your light
I can think clearly because of your light
All my cares are dealt with because of your light

My heart is full of love because of your light
Things always work out for me because of your light
My power and confidence is because of your light
All my successes are because of your light
All my acts of kindness are because of your light
All my words of inspiration are because of your light
Everything in my world functions because of your light
I feel loved and cared for because of your light
I feel my own power because of your light
I have nothing to give to anyone without your light
My eyes can see because of your light
My heart beats because of your light
Dear God thank you for your love and light

Word of the day

Gift

www.zmahoon.com

28. Gift

Thank you Dear God for this beautiful new day
I love waking up to sunshine and clear blue skies
I love waking up feeling happy and relaxed
Thank you for the gift of life
It is a gift that has so many other gifts within it
My physical body is my biggest gift
I am in awe of the systems in my body that function effortlessly

My eyes are a wonderful gift, helping me see far and wide
Helping me to see color and depth and shapes
Much of my enjoyment of life comes from being able to see the beauty of the world around me
Each thing I feast my eyes on is a gift – the flowers, the clouds, the mountains, the trees
The beauty of all of nature is a gift
Thank you Dear God for the precious gift of sight

My ears are a wonderful gift, helping me hear the delightful sound of running water and chirping birds
I love listening to music of all different types, music in itself is a gift
I love the peace and tranquility of silence too
Thank you Dear God for the gift of hearing

I so appreciate the gift of taste, being able to enjoy foods of all sorts
I love tasting my morning coffee, it gets me energized for my day
I love tasting the different ways food is cooked from all over the world
I love tasting fruits and experimenting with spices
My sense of taste is a wonderful gift

The ability of my body to take whatever I give it and extract what it needs to nourish and replenish is a gift that I really appreciate
It is wonderful that my body can function without my conscious involvement
I love knowing that; I love knowing that my body is a precious gift
Thank you Dear God for this amazing gift
A gift that is there for me every day of my existence on Earth
A gift that is versatile and agile; a gift that enables me to move around and do things
A gift that enables me to define my preferences
A gift that enables me to derive so much joy and satisfaction from life

Thank you Dear God for the gift of love
My children are my biggest gift, they help me to flow love and find joy in little things
My parents are a gift, for they gave me the stability I needed to find my place in the world
My friends are a gift, for they provide me with many happy times and different perspectives
My colleagues are a gift for they make my work easy and enjoyable
My clients are a gift for they create opportunities for my creativity to flow and grow
My talents and abilities are a gift for they give me so much satisfaction and joy
My health is a gift, and I want more of that
My prosperity is a gift, and I want more of that
I have the gift of words, being able to express myself in many different ways
I have the gift of creativity, being able to present what I know in ways that makes it easy for others to understand and adopt
I have the gift of drawing upon Source for knowledge and flowing it whenever I want

I have the gift of being able to learn and grow and being happy with myself
I have the gift of light heartedness and love, bringing joy to the lives of everyone around me
All the teachers I have met and the things I have learnt from them have been gifts that came to me at the right time and place, and I am so appreciative of them all
Each day that I can enjoy these gifts is a gift that I am thankful for
Thank you Dear God for all my gifts. I appreciate each and every one of them, and I want many more gifts to flow into my life on a consistent daily basis. I love you. I love life.

Word of the day

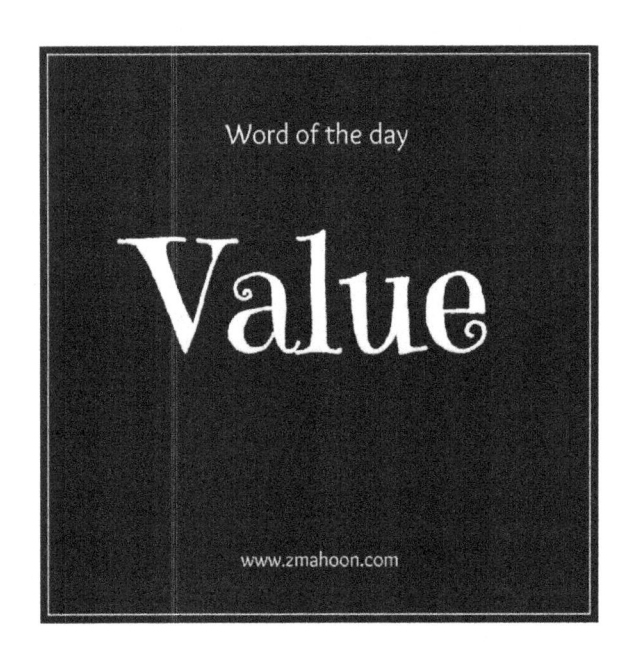

Value

www.zmahoon.com

29. Value

Dear God, Thank you for another day of joy
Today I want to look for things to appreciate
I know that there are countless things, people and events of value in the world
And I know that it is easy for me to find things to appreciate
I know that there is value in everything

There is value in the sun that shines and warms the Earth
There is value in changing seasons, the wind, the rain and the snow
There is value in the trees and plants and flowers that grow
There is value in the many different life forms that inhabit the Earth
There is value in the earth worms and the butterflies
There is value in the mice and the elephants
There is value in the oceans and the deserts
There is value in the night and day
There is value in the jungles and the farm lands
There is value in the cities and the towns
There is value in a candle and a light bulb
There is value in new things and old
There is value in different professions and different people
There is value in doing things in different ways

I am one who looks for value in everything and everyone
When something good happens I appreciate the value of that
And when something I don't understand happens I look for the value in that
I acknowledge that there are many things that I don't always understand
I acknowledge that I don't always see the value in things right away
But I know that things always work out for me
Therefore there is value in all my experiences

Just because I can't see the value at times, doesn't mean it isn't there
Everything in my world reflects my point of attraction and therefore it is guidance and it is of value
When things work the way I want them to, that is a valuable indicator
And when things don't work quite the way I want them to that too is a valuable indicator

I am happy to give every person and every situation the benefit of the doubt
I am happy to keep open expectations about everything
I am happy to allow the value of things and people to unfold
I am happy knowing that when I expect good things good things come about
I am happy knowing that when I see everything as having value then I create value
I want to feel my own value
I want to feel that I am of value to others
I want to feel that my presence in this world makes a difference
I want to feel that I am creating value every day and that when I leave I will leave value behind
I want to feel the value of everything I do and everyone I meet
I want to feel the value of living life to the max
I want to feel the value of each moment of everyday
Thank you Dear God for this valuable gift of life. I love you. I love life.

Word of the day

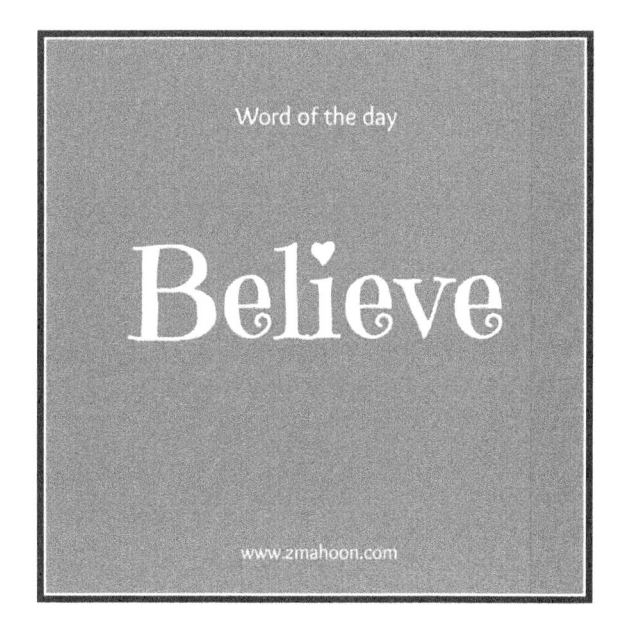

Believe

www.zmahoon.com

30. Believe

Thank you God for another day to enjoy life
I love the feeling of being alive
I love the feeling of being relaxed and happy
I believe that I can be relaxed and happy every day
I believe in the powerful law of attraction
I believe that I am a powerful creator
I believe that I can create deliberately by thinking consciously
I believe that I can choose my thoughts and that what I choose has an impact on my future
I believe that thinking positive thoughts will bring me things that make me happy
I believe that I'm beginning to know how to think positively

I acknowledge that there is a difference between wanting positive results and thinking positively
I want to be one who knows how to think positively
I want to be one who chooses thoughts deliberately
I want to be one who creates a happy day every day
I want to feel the ease and flow of life
I want to feel freedom and joy
I want to feel love and appreciation
I believe that I can choose what to believe and that whatever I believe creates my life experience – my reality
I choose to believe that the world is a friendly place
I choose to believe that the contrast of this world helps me to identify my preferences and that is a good thing
I choose to believe that God loves me and is always guiding me towards the things I want
I choose to believe that I can have, be or do anything I want because I have guidance

I choose to believe that I can trust my guidance on all things; I can trust the way I feel
I choose to believe that when I feel good I am lined up with the object of my desire
I choose to believe that I can tell the difference between being lined up and not
I choose to believe that I know what to do to get lined up
I have evidence of my own that proves to me the power of my thoughts
I have evidence that proves to me that my beliefs are at the basis of the way I experience the world

I believe that I can change the way I experience the world by changing my beliefs
I want to choose those beliefs that lead to my freedom and joy
And I am ready to give up all those beliefs that no longer serve me
I believe that everyone is like me; we are all the same
I believe that we are all extensions of Source, and that which we call God
I believe that we are all love at our core and we all want the same things
We all want love, freedom, joy and prosperity
I believe that the powerful law of attraction can give us each what we want
I believe that I am one who loves and I am the happiest when I love
I love myself and I love all my co-creators, I love creation
I believe that anything is possible
I believe that miracles are a way of life
I believe that I can live each day with joy and end each day with satisfaction
And that is what I want

Today I want to live each moment with joy
I want to end this day feeling happy and satisfied, at peace with myself and with the world
Thank you God for helping me understand the power of my beliefs. I love being a deliberate creator. I love you. I love life.

Word of the day

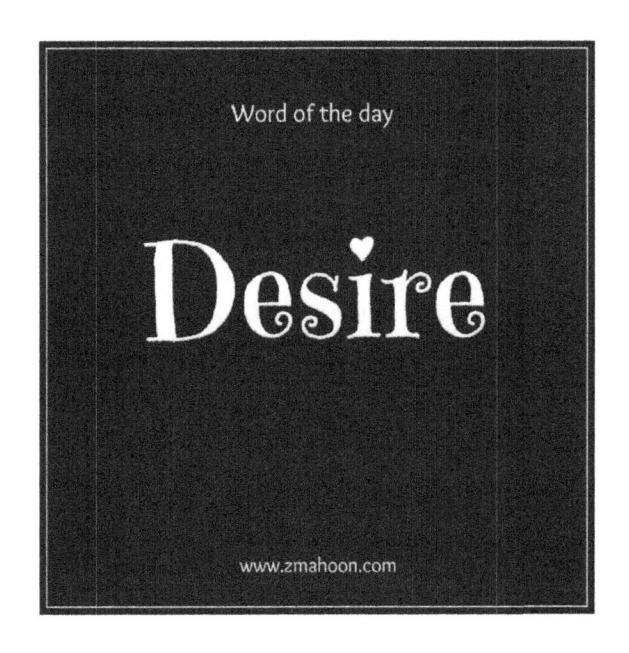

Desire

www.zmahoon.com

31. Desire

Dear God, thank you for this wonderful new day
Today I feel alive with the feeling of desire pulsating within me
I have many desires that are pulling me
I desire wellbeing for myself and for others
I desire the wellbeing of this beautiful planet
I desire the wellbeing of all living things
The animals, the plants, the seas, the mountains and the plains
I desire the wellbeing of the people in my life

My children, my family, my friends, and all those who co-create with me
My desire is to see them all thrive in every moment of every day
My desire is to feel my own wellbeing, and to know it with certainty
My desire is to be free to choose what I want
My desire is to follow my bliss and feel the ease and flow of life
My desire is to always have something to laugh about and celebrate
My desire is to feel the energy and vitality of my physical body
My desire is to always listen for my guidance and follow it
My desire is to always have more things to want, more to get out of life and every day

Life is good when there is something to look forward to – something to desire
It is my desire to allow prosperity to flow
It is my desire to find ways to spend money on enjoyable things
It is my desire to always have all my desires fulfilled easily
It is my desire to feel my abundance and prosperity and to find evidence of it everyday
It is my desire to enjoy my work and the company of the people I work with

It is my desire to end each day feeling happy and satisfied with my accomplishments
It is my desire to always do my best
It is my desire to be of value to others and to feel my own value
It is my desire to flow love and joy
It is my desire to receive love and co-create in harmony and joy
It is my desire to be happy
It is fun to desire new things
New places to explore, new things to try
New things to buy
New friends to meet

Desire is what makes life so interesting
I love knowing that whatever I desire is possible
I love knowing that the moment I give birth to a desire it is given
I love knowing that all I have to do is to relax to let it into my life experience
I love knowing that it is not my job to think about how it will come, and who will bring it and when it will happen
I love knowing that I can be lighthearted about it all
I love knowing that contrast and variety help me to give birth to new desires
I love knowing that I will always have more to desire
I love the feeling of desire – it makes me feel alive

Thank you God for the variety of this world that helps me to define my preferences and continue giving birth to desires
I understand now that the purpose of birthing desire is to have fun and not to get anything done
I understand that my work is to give birth to desires and I can let you look after their manifestation
Thank you Dear God for the wonderful life I am living. I love you. I love life.

Word of the day

Pleasure

www.zmahoon.com

32. Pleasure

Dear God, Thank you for a brand new day
Today I want to extract as much pleasure as I can from every moment of my day
When I feel the feeling of pleasure and joy, I am in a place of allowing
When I feel the feeling of pleasure and joy, I know that I am on my way to more pleasure and joy
I love feeling pleasure and joy
There are so many things that give me pleasure

Today I want to feel my way to pleasure
Today I want to appreciate my way to pleasure
Today I want to love my way to pleasure
Today I want to dance my way to pleasure
Today I want to breathe my way to pleasure
Today I want to sing my way to pleasure
Today I want to find many ways to get to the feeling of pleasure

Watching a baby play gives me pleasure
Listening to children laugh gives me pleasure
Looking at flowers blooming gives me pleasure
Gazing at trees gives me pleasure
Listening to the sound of the little brook gives me pleasure
Watching the clouds float by gives me pleasure
Looking at snow covered mountain peaks gives me pleasure
Talking to good friends gives me pleasure
Driving on an open road gives me pleasure
Letting the breeze blow on my face and through my hair gives me pleasure
The gentle rocking of a boat gives me pleasure
The sun warming my back gives me pleasure

Tasting good food gives me pleasure
Cooking good food gives me pleasure
Having others enjoy good food gives me pleasure
Reading a good book gives me pleasure
Watching movies with my children gives me pleasure
Taking a nap in the afternoon gives me pleasure
Writing and journaling gives me pleasure
Watching a the fire burn in my fireplace gives me pleasure
I am so blessed because my life is full of things that give me pleasure
It is so easy for me to find something that gives me pleasure to appreciate
Thank you God for allowing me so many opportunities for appreciation and pleasure
I love my life. I love me. I love the feeling of pleasure.

Word of the day

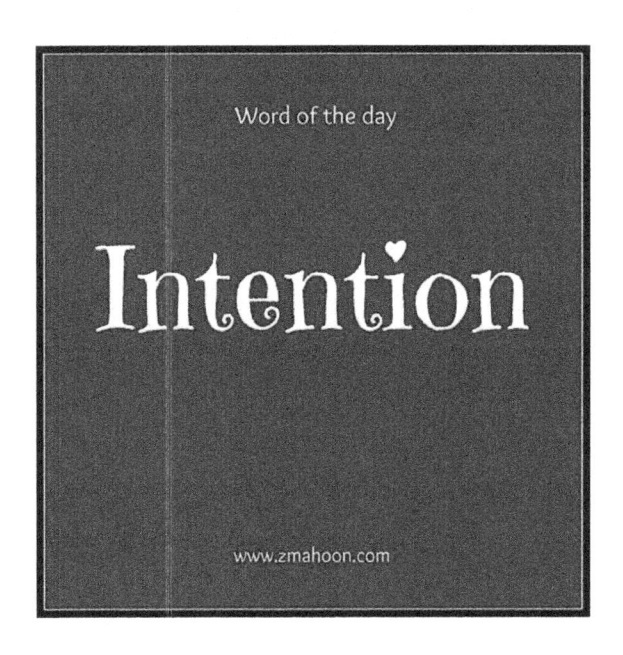

Intention

www.zmahoon.com

33. Intention

Dear God, Thank you for this beautiful new day
It is my intention to make the most of this wonderful day
It is my intention to look for things to appreciate
It is my intention to find joy in little things
It is my intention to love myself
It is my intention to be loving to all
It is my intention to listen for my guidance
It is my intention to look for signs that help guide me
It is my intention to look for things that feel good
It is my intention to do my best
It is my intention to end this day feeling happy and satisfied
It is my intention to have fun

Thank you for showing me that my intention paves the way to my manifestations
My intention is just a decision to give attention to something with the objective of bringing it to me
I know that my intention is the thing that creates the pull of desire
I know now that I must have clear intentions about what I want
I know now that my intentions and my beliefs must be aligned
Today it is my intention to give up all the beliefs that no longer serve me
Today I intend to use my power of focus consciously and deliberately
Today I intend to focus on those things that make me happy

I know that when I am happy I am allowing my guidance
I know that when I am happy all my intentions are being fulfilled
I know that being happy is a decision
I know that all intentions are like decisions
When I intend something, I have decided that I want it

Today it is my intention to consciously give my attention to those beliefs that serve my purpose
I intend prosperity and I declare that abundance is the norm of the universe
I intend good health and I declare that my body always knows what to do to be healthy
I intend loving relationships and I declare that the love I give is what is reflected back to me in all my relationships
I intend ease and flow in everything I do and I declare that life is as easy as I let it be
I intend joyous co-creation and I declare that when I look for joy I always find it
I intend to live life fully and happily and I declare that things always work out for me
I intend to be unconditionally loving and I declare that being unconditional is my natural state
I intend to thrive in every way and I declare that I was born to thrive
I intend to have, be and do anything I want, and I declare that it is possible, not only possible but certain

My happiness is certain
My success is certain
My prosperity is certain
My health is certain
My joyous co-creation with others is certain
My wellbeing is certain
The love of God is certain.
I love you Dear God. I love me. I love life.

Word of the day

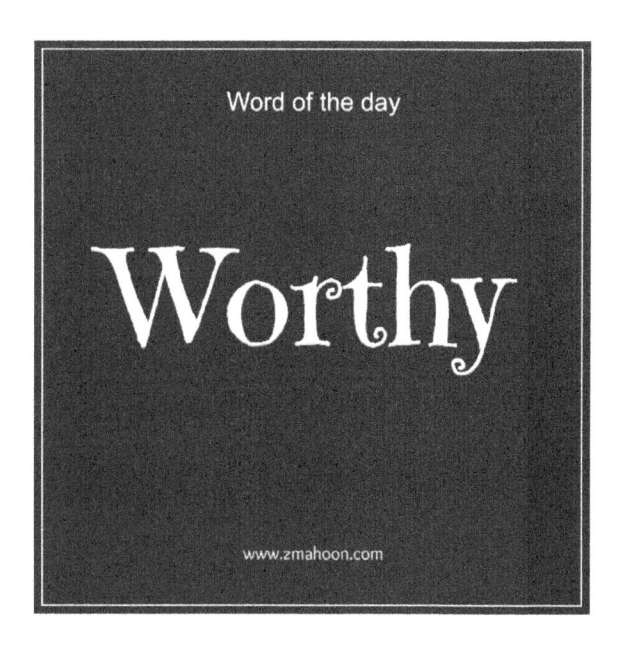

Worthy

www.zmahoon.com

34. Worthy

Thank you God for another beautiful day
Thank you for the blessings that you keep sending my way
Thank you for the love that fills my every day
Thank you for the guidance that is always there for me
Thank you for the knowing that sets my spirit free
Thank you for the many wonderful gifts that make me feel truly worthy
Thank you for my children, my home and my country
Today I want to feel my worthiness and value
Today I want to look at the world as if it were brand new

I know that when I feel worthy I send love to me
I know that when I feel worthy I send love to you
I know that when I feel worthy I feel happy for others
I know that when I feel worthy all good things come to me
Feeling worthy really is at the basis of all well-being
When I feel worthy I feel one with the energy of the Universe
When I feel worthy I feel that anything is possible
When I feel worthy I know my place in the world
When I feel worthy I feel confident and happy
When I feel worthy I know that things are always working out for me
When I feel worthy I appreciate the contrast of this world
When I feel worthy I feel like flowing love to everyone and everything around me
I love the feeling of worthiness

As I begin to understand that my every wish is important
And that my thoughts have the power to create
I begin to feel my worthiness and Your love for me
It feels good to know how important I am

It feels good to know that I have value
It feels good to know that You want me to thrive
It feels good to know that You are always sending me guidance to help me
It feels good to know that I am not only deserving but I am worthy beyond measure
It feels good to know that this world and everything in it is here for my enjoyment
It feels good to know that I am free to choose what I want
It feels good to know that I have the power to change my life whenever I want
It feels good to know that I am unlimited
It feels good to know that I can have, be or do anything I want
It feels good to know that my power of creation is completely under my control
It feels good to know that nothing can ever go wrong, that all is always well
It feels good to know that You Dear God never withdraw your love from me
It feels good to know that I too can be one who flows love unconditionally
It feels good to know that my worthiness and my value are a given thing
It feels good to know that I do not have to earn my worthiness or my value

Thank you Dear God for always making me feel loved
I want to feel your love everyday
I want to feel my worthiness everyday
Thank you Dear God for your love. I love you. I love my life. I love me.

Word of the day

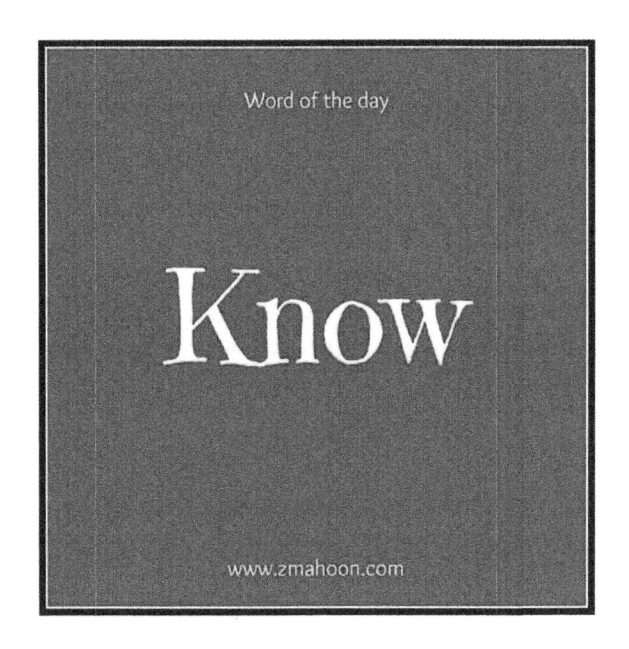

Know

www.zmahoon.com

35. Know

Dear God, thank you for another opportunity to enjoy life
Thank you for the abundance that is flowing so freely into my life
I love the feeling of looking forward with eager anticipation
I love the feeling of being in the flow
I know that things always work out for me
I know that You Dear God are always leading me towards my wellbeing
I know that all I have to do is to relax and have fun
I know that I am learning to relax and have more fun
I know that I am happier now than I have ever been before
I know that my life just keeps getting better and better and better
I know that I am learning to trust
I know that trust is the answer
I know that I can be like a tree and allow everything I want to come to me
I know that my life is reflecting back to me what I am doing with my thoughts

I know that I am doing very well for I have come a long way
I know that I get it now; I understand how to think my thoughts on purpose
And I know that I get a little better at it everyday
I can feel the peace within my being
I can feel the joy of waking up to a brand new day

I know the power of appreciation and meditation
I know the power of taking the easy way
I know that I am a powerful creator
I know that I am unlimited
I know that I can have, be or do anything I want
I know that the future is mine
I know that this is my time

This is my time to shine
This is my time to live life to the max
This is my time to receive all the things I have been asking for
Thank you Dear God for everything you have given me
I love you. I love life. I love me!

Word of the day

Wisdom

www.zmahoon.com

36. Wisdom

Dear God, Thank you for this wonderful new day
Today I am reaching for wisdom and understanding
Today I am reaching for connection with the Source of all knowledge
I know that genius is the ability to flow wisdom from that Source
And the Source of all wisdom is God

I want to bring the wisdom of God into everything I do
I want to bring the wisdom of God into every thought I think
I want to bring the wisdom of God into everything I feel
I want to bring the wisdom of God into every moment of my life
I want to bring the wisdom of God into every decision I make
I want to be consciously aware of God's wisdom and remember that I can trust it at all times

Nothing anyone has every accomplished can parallel the wisdom of God
So it makes sense to trust that wisdom and let it guide me
I see evidence of God's wisdom all around me
There is wisdom in the balance of the world
There is wisdom in the cycle of life and death
There is wisdom in the laws of physics
There is wisdom in every chemical reaction
There is wisdom in the existence of every living thing
There is wisdom in the way day follows night
There is wisdom in the changing of the seasons
There is wisdom in the contrast between sweet and salty
There is wisdom in the rain and snow
There is wisdom in the seed that gives birth to the tree
There is wisdom in the depths of the ocean
There is wisdom in the far reaches of the sky

There is wisdom in the way my body functions
There is wisdom in the process of creation
There is wisdom in every co-creation

I love knowing that I have access to God's wisdom
I love knowing that I can align with the frequency of love and draw on the Source of all wisdom
I love knowing that all my decisions are easy because I have access to that wisdom
I love knowing that I am always connected to the Source of that wisdom
I love knowing that I don't have to figure anything out

My job is to allow God's wisdom to lead me to what is best
My job is to observe, enjoy and define preferences
And trust in God's wisdom to bring me all that is best for me
I trust God's wisdom and I surrender to it
I can feel that my life is much easier when I trust God's wisdom
I can feel that I make better decisions when I trust God's wisdom
I can feel that God's wisdom is always there for me, guiding me, helping me, supporting me, showing me, assisting me, calling me, loving me on my way.
Thank you dear God for the guidance that is always there for me. I love you. I love life.

Word of the day

Marvel

www.zmahoon.com

37. Marvel

Dear God, Thank you for this marvelous new day
Today I am in awe of what You have created
Today I marvel at the intricacy of the Universe
The planets, and the solar system, the stars and the galaxies
I marvel at how smoothly the sun rises and sets each day
I marvel at the ebb and flow of the waters
I marvel at the diversity of living things on Earth
I marvel at the beautiful trees of so many different shapes and sizes
I marvel at the amazing colors of flowers and butterflies
I marvel at how water turns to clouds and then to rain and snow
I marvel at the changing weather and the contrast it creates
I marvel at the little ants and their colonies and their role in creation
And the bees and their hives and how they make honey
I marvel at the geese always knowing where they are going
I marvel at all animals and their instinctive knowing
I marvel at how a little seed gives birth to a big tree
And how a tiny egg gives birth to big bird
I marvel at how my body functions without my knowing
I marvel at all the things that have to happen to allow me to see
And all the things that have to happen to allow me to feel, and taste and touch
Hear and smell

I marvel at how complex all the systems in my body are
And how easy it is for You to create them and keep them going
Life truly is a marvelous gift
The world truly is a magnificent place to live
I marvel at the science behind light and sound, heat and power
And countless things yet to be discovered

I marvel at the variety I have to choose from
I marvel at the scores delicious fruits and nuts
And the different tasting vegetables
The seeds and spices and herbs that make it fun to cook
I marvel at the beauty of the vistas and waterfalls
And the mountains and the plains
I marvel at the perfection of all creation
And the beauty of it all

I marvel at what people can achieve and create
I marvel at the miracle of life
There are so many ways in which You keep showing me that anything is possible
There is so much evidence in this world of Your power and wisdom

I love knowing that I have access to Your power and wisdom
I love knowing that everything in this world is for me to enjoy
I love knowing that all I have to do is to marvel at creation and to appreciate it
I love knowing that as I marvel at creation I step into my power
I love knowing that I am the creator and I am the creation
I love knowing that many marvelous things happen when I trust your guidance
I love knowing that my life is marvelous in many ways

Thank you Dear God for creating this Universe and all the marvelous things in it. I love all of it.
I love you. I love life.

Word of the day

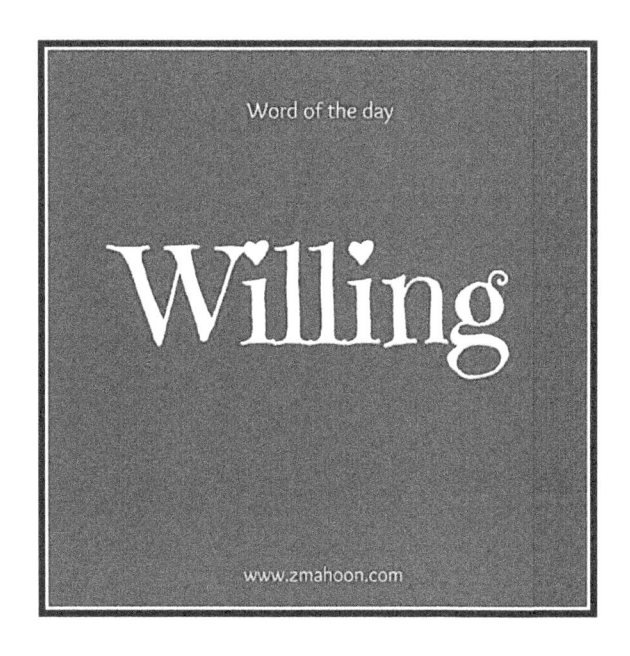

Willing

www.zmahoon.com

38. Willing

Dear God Thank you for this wonderful new day
Today I am willing to see the good in everything that comes before me
I feel happy as I look out on to the world
Fall colors warm my heart and make me smile
What a beautiful place I live in, thank you for this

I have decided to be open and willing today
Today I am willing to listen to my inner guidance
Today I am willing to go where I am called to go and do what I am called to do
Today I am willing to give people a chance, I am willing to conscoiusly look for and find something about them that I can appreciate
Today I am willing to be kind to people
I am willing to be generous
Today I am willing to love and be loved
Today I am willing to be kind to myself
I am willing to allow myself to be who I am and who I want to be
Today I am willing to believe in my dreams
Today I am willing to believe that all things are truly possible
I am willing to believe in your power to make it so
Today I am willing to believe that there is good in everything
Today I am willing to keep an open mind
Today I am willing to keep judgement at bay
Today I am willing to allow joy, and create joy

I am willing to find joy in little things like the pretty colors and shapes of flowers that are still abloom
I am willing to smile more and laugh more
I am willing to extend warmth and love to everyone around me

I am willing for adventure, I am willing for excitement
I am willing to allow things to unfold naturally
I am willing to relax because I know you are in control so I don't need to be
Today I am willing to appreciate the little girl with the big smile I saw on the street

And the children walking happily to school
And my puppy licking my face
And my cats purring
And my children enjoying a deep sleep
And my morning coffee
And the place where I live

The warmth and coziness of my home
The friends who are always there for me
The possibilities that are fun to think about
The newness of a rain washed world
The freshness of crisp morning breeze

Today I am willing to let you have your way Dear God
Today I am willing to be guided
Today I am willing to see what you want me to see and hear what you want me to hear and go where you want me to go
Today I am willing to just be me
I love you Dear God, I love life and I am willing to allow all good things to flow to me.

Word of the day

Vibration

www.zmahoon.com

39. Vibration

Dear God, Thank you for this beautiful new day
Today I am full of life, full of energy and vitality
It is going to be a good day today
Today I want to find unison with the vibration of the universe

I understand that each word I think has vibration
I understand that I can consciously choose words with a positive vibration
I know that this is what deliberate creation is all about
I know that when I vibrate joy, good things happen
I know that when I vibrate love, I receive love
I know that when I vibrate prosperity, I attract more prosperity
I know that when I vibrate health, my body responds to me
I want to hold my vibration constant in a place of love and joy
I want to feel my vibration and use it as my guide

Today I want to choose thoughts that feel good
I know that thoughts that feel good have more power
Today I want my positive vibration to influence everyone around me
Today I want my positive vibration to bring me new possibilities
Today I want my now vibration to create a better future
Today is my day, Dear God
Today is my day for all good things to come to me
Today I am vibrating with my higher power
Today I am in harmony with that which I consider to be good
Today I am allowing my wellbeing to flow to me
Today I am in sync with the vibration of the Universe

Today I am vibrating love
Today I am vibrating success

Today I am vibrating prosperity
Today I am vibrating health
Today I am vibrating joy
Today I am vibrating freedom
Today I am vibrating creativity
Today is my day to feel good
Today I can feel my alignment
Today I can feel my allowing
Today I can feel my guidance
Thank you Dear God for all the good things in my life. I love you. I love life.

Word of the day

Wish...

www.zmahoon.com

40. Wish

Dear God, Thank you for this brand new day
Today I wish for peace around the world
I wish for joy, and abundance and health for everyone

My wish is to see smiles on all faces
My wish is to see all hearts fulfilled
My wish is to see beauty all around me
My wish is to see people in love
My wish is to see the sun rise and shine all over the Earth
My wish is to see green fields and golden crops and big old trees everywhere

My wish is to see tall peaks and deep oceans
My wish is to see love and prosperity among all nations
My wish is to see people glowing with joy
My wish is to see comfort and harmony in all homes
My wish is to feel love surround the Earth
My wish is to find peace with my heart
My wish is to feel free as the breeze
My wish is to love and be loved

My wish is to live and be present in each moment of everyday
My wish is to teach through the power of my own experience
My wish is to keep learning and growing
My wish is to extend a helping hand
My wish is to have a tender heart
My wish is to keep an open mind
My wish is to be the best I can
My wish is to trust and have faith

My wish is to feel God's love
My wish is to always know my guidance
My wish to travel an easy path
My wish is to be who I am
My wish is to know my true power
My wish is to feel confident
My wish is to feel worthy of all good things
My wish is that everyone reading my wishes add their power to mine
My wish is that all my wishes come true

Thank you God for all the wellbeing that keeps the balance of this world
Thank you God for all the people who strive for excellence in many ways
Thank you God for the continuity of life
Thank you God for who I am and who I am becoming
I love you. I love life.

Word of the day

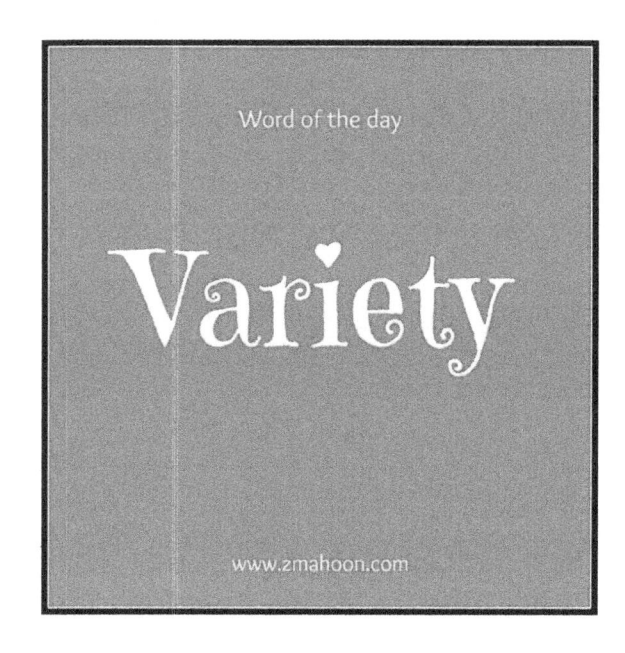

Variety

www.zmahoon.com

41. Variety

Dear God, Thank you for this wonderful new day
Today I am focusing on the variety that I have to choose from
There is so much variety in everything
I know that as I appreciate variety, I feel good
And when I feel good more good comes my way
Today I will appreciate variety where ever I can
I can choose from a variety of things to eat
I love that there is so much variety of foods in the world
And so much variety in the way we cook
I love the variety of spices and herbs
I love the variety of how food can look
I love the colors and the aromas

Variety is what makes it possible for me to choose what I prefer
And I love that
I love that I can define what I really, really want and variety is the tool that helps me come to that awareness
I love the variety of different colors and styles to wear
I love the variety of different cars to drive
I love the variety of different books to read
I love the variety of different music to listen to
I love the variety of places to go to and things to do
I love the variety of trying out new games to play
I love the variety of meeting new people
I love the variety of different languages spoken around the world
I love the variety of customs and traditions
I love the variety of fruits to eat and things to cook
I love the variety of experiences I have had in life that have taught me so much

I love the variety of teachers I have had in the past and their wisdom
I love the variety of friends I have and the different things I appreciate about them
I love the variety of places I've been to and things I've seen
I love the variety of creativity around the planet
I love that no two people are the same
I love that no two pictures are the same
I love that no two places are the same
I love that no two moments in time are the same
I love the variety of my life
I love that I am one who creates variety where there is none
I love that I can change where I live and what I do
I love that I can change the paint on my walls and the furniture in my room
I love that I can change everything about my life
I love that I can change Me!
I love that I love variety, it makes my life easy

When I accept variety I go with the flow more
When I accept variety I am open to change
When I accept variety life is fun
I don't just accept variety, I look for it
I look for new things to feast my eyes on
I look for new things to enjoy
I love trusting that there will be a variety of ways for me to get what I want
I thrive on variety
Variety is the spice of life
Variety makes life fun and interesting
Dear God, Thank you for the variety in my life. I love variety. I love you. I love life.

Word of the day

Good

www.zmahoon.com

42. Good

Dear God, Thank you for another day that's going to be really, really good
Today I want to feel really, really good
I know that when I feel good I have a good day
Today I want to choose those thoughts that make me feel good when I think them
I acknowledge that I don't need things to change to feel good
But when I feel good, things change and become better

I am learning that I can feel good whenever I want to
Whether I feel good about the past or the present or the future
I am doing it all Now – and now is where all my power is
When I feel good in each now moment, I am creating a good life
Thoughts of appreciation are thoughts that feel good

When I think of how blessed I am, I feel good
When I think of how much I have going for me, I feel good
When I feel the vitality of my physical body, I feel good
When I look at my children I feel good
When I bask in the sunshine, I feel good
When I taste delicious food, I feel good
When I go wading in a stream, I feel good
When I sit under a tree, I feel good

Today I will look for thoughts and things that make me feel good
I can always find something to appreciate about the people that I meet
I can always find something to appreciate about my work
I can always find something to appreciate about myself
I love looking at things with the expectation of finding the good in them
When I expect good things, good things happen

Things always work out for me
Good things always come my way
I am learning to allow good things to flow
I am learning to allow myself to feel good
There is so much to feel good about each day

When I feel good, I am in harmony with all that is good
When I feel good, I flow love to all those around me
When I feel good, my work seems easy
When I feel good, I have perfect timing
When I feel good, I use perfect words
When I feel good, I make people laugh
When I feel good, I laugh
When I feel good, I see so much more to appreciate
When I feel good, life feels good

There is power in feeling good
There is joy in feeling good
I want to feel good
Thank you Dear God for a good feeling day. I aim to make the best of this day. I aim to feel good.
I love you. I love life.

Word of the day

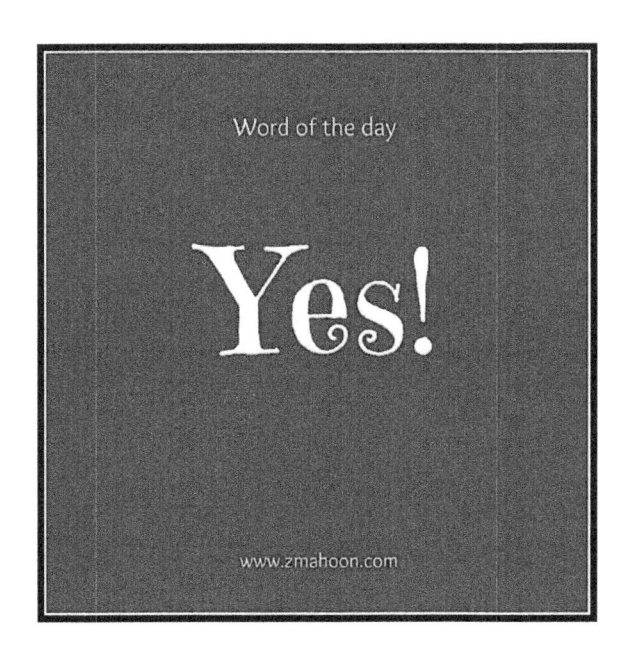

Yes!

www.zmahoon.com

43. Yes!

Dear God, Thank you for this beautiful new day
I love waking up feeling happy and refreshed
I love the feeling of being alive and well

Today, I want to shout "yes!" as loud as I can
"Yes" to joy
"Yes" to wellbeing
"Yes" to abundance
"Yes" to love
"Yes" to beauty
"Yes" to all good things coming my way

I know now that "yes" is the easy way
When I say "yes" I am going with the flow
When I say "yes" I am allowing You to guide me
When I say "yes" I am trusting that whatever comes is good for me
When I say "yes" I am in harmony with the universe
When I say "yes" I feel the ease and flow of life
When I say "yes" my path opens up to new possibilities
When I say "yes" I feel movement forward
When I say "yes" I feel clarity and decisiveness
When I say "yes" I feel the power of commitment
Life is easy when I say yes to whatever comes my way

Yes, Yes, Yes, Yes, Yes
Yes, I am ready to choose joy today
Yes, I am ready to choose love
Yes, I am ready to choose peace
Yes, I am ready to have fun

Yes, I am ready to enjoy
Yes, I am ready to laugh
Yes, I am ready to appreciate
Yes, I am ready to be happy
Yes, I am ready to step into my true power
Yes, I am ready to be loving
Yes, I am ready to allow my creativity to flow
Yes, I am ready to enjoy co-creation
Yes, I am ready to think on purpose and create on purpose
Yes, I am ready, I am ready for this journey

Yes, my life is good
Yes, I feel blessed
Yes, I am a powerful creator
Yes, I am unlimited
Yes, I can have, be or do anything I want
Yes, I am here
Yes, I am ready to be guided
Yes, Dear God I am ready and listening to your guidance
Thank you for all my blessings. I love you. I love life.

Word of the day

Thrive!

www.zmahoon.com

44. Thrive

Dear God, Thank you for this beautiful exhilarating day
I feel full of life today
I feel energized
I feel ready to do more
I feel happy and alive
I feel ready to thrive!
Thriving is the feeling of energy moving
Thriving is the feeling of allowing
I am beginning to understand that thriving means reaching for joy
Today I want to thrive in many ways

I want to feel the feeling of thriving, the feeling of allowing energy to flow
I feel that feeling when I am in a place of allowing
I thrive when money flows in
I thrive when I spend money
I thrive when I love
I thrive when I receive love
I thrive when I feel healthy
I thrive when I feel confident
I thrive when I laugh
I thrive when I do things that are fun to do
I thrive when I co-create in harmony with others
I thrive when I look at beautiful things and appreciate them

Appreciation is the key to thriving
The more I appreciate the more I thrive
And there are so many things in this world for me to appreciate
I appreciate the pure white snow on the ground and I thrive
I appreciate the cheerful happy sunshine and I thrive

I appreciate the snow clad trees and I thrive
I appreciate my warm mug of coffee and I thrive
I appreciate the happy children playing in the snow and I thrive
I appreciate my cat sitting in my lap to purr and I thrive
I appreciate the friends and co-creators who draw out the best of me and I thrive
I appreciate the friends and co-creators who let me draw out the best of them and I thrive
I appreciate the work I do and I thrive
I appreciate my beautiful house and I thrive
I appreciate the strength and stamina of my physical body and I thrive
I appreciate those who love me and I thrive
I appreciate those I love and I thrive

All of creation meant for me to appreciate, meant to help me thrive
When I thrive my life is fun
When I thrive my life feels of value
When I thrive I feel good
And when I feel good I thrive
I can always thrive because I can always reach for a thought that feels good
Today I want to focus on feeling good
Today I will find things to appreciate
Today I will most certainly thrive
Thank you Dear God for this wonderful day with so many opportunities to thrive and become more and feel good. I love you. I love life.

Word of the day

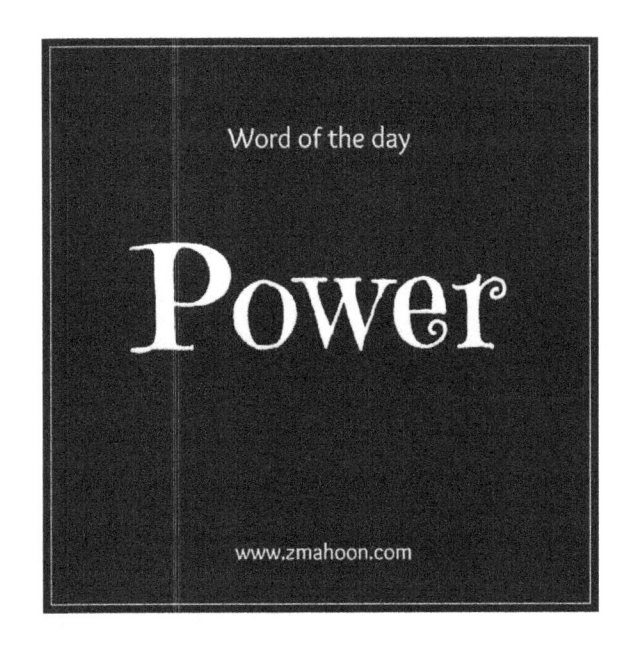

Power

www.zmahoon.com

45. Power

Dear God, Thank you for this powerful new day
Today is going to be an amazing day
Today I will focus on making the best of every moment
I know that my power lies in being present in the now
Because now is when I am creating what will come next
I know that I am a powerful creator, and each thought I think is important
Each thought I think has power
I want to direct my power towards things that I want
I want more fun, more freedom and more finances
I want more love, more delicious experiences, more wellbeing
Today I want to step into my power and use it wisely
I have the power to create my own reality

I feel my power when things I think about come to pass easily without my conscious involvement
I feel my power when people are nice to me
I feel my power when I am nice to them
I feel my power when I have a knowing inside me that all is well
I feel my power when I am in touch with my guidance
I feel my power when things turn out exactly the way I want them to
I feel my power when money flows into my life with ease and flow
I feel my power when things line-up for me in surprising ways
I feel my power when I enjoy the agility and stamina of my body
I feel my power when I close my eyes and meditate
I can feel my power in so many way and it feels good

I acknowledge that the power I feel is the power I draw from You Dear God
I acknowledge that when I am lined-up I am an extension of You

I acknowledge that what I call my power is really Your power flowing through me
I acknowledge that Your power is the power that creates worlds
I acknowledge that I am the happiest when I allow that power to flow through me
I acknowledge that I am the object of You loving attention and guidance

Thank you for everything you have blessed me with Dear God
I love feeling the energy of your power flowing through me
Today I want to allow that flow at full force
I want to end this day feeling satisfied with myself and my accomplishments
I want to end this day feeling and knowing that I am a powerful creator
I want to end this day knowing that all is well
I want to end this day with clarity
I want to end this day feeling the joy of being alive
I want to end this day feeling the perfection of my being
Thank you God for the power you have given me. I love my power to create. I love you. I love life.

Word of the day

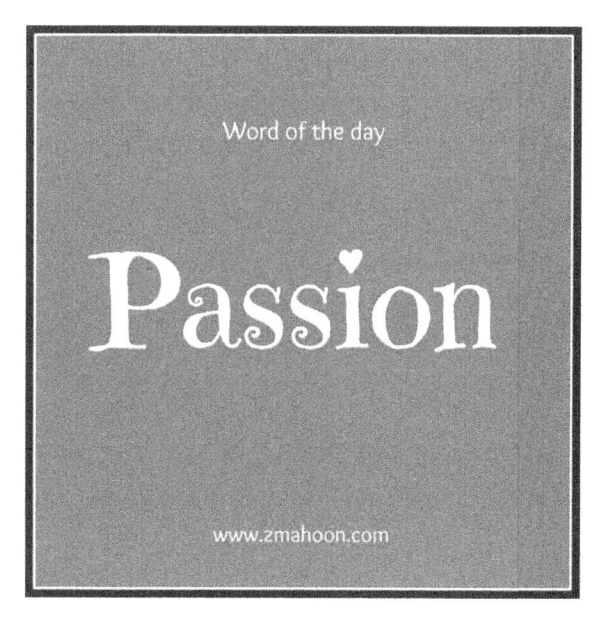

Passion

www.zmahoon.com

46. Passion

Dear God, Thank you for this wonderful new day
My word for today is "passion"
Today I want to feel the feeling of passion – the feeling of energy moving at full speed

Passion feels like a song in my heart
Passion feels like the thrill of certainty
Passion feels like the pounding of my pulse
Passion feels like heightened wanting coupled with joy
Passion is the feeling of enjoying the journey when I know that success is certain
Passion is the feeling of waking up in the morning and jumping out of bed because I can't wait to get started
Passion is the feeling of waking up with the feeling of power
Passion is the feeling of a tidal wave of love pouring from my being
That is how I feel today – I feel my power, I feel my passion

I feel an immeasurable passion for life – my life
I know that the way I am feeling is what is making the world seem different to me today
I feel as if the colors are brighter, the sky is bluer than blue, the trees are greener than green
Everything seems so much more beautiful than ever before
I feel like I am seeing the world through the eyes of God, and it looks perfect beyond words
Everything is perfect, and my heart is singing with joy
Today I feel passionate about being alive
I feel passionate about moving about the world in my physical body and enjoying that

I feel passionate about enjoying really good food, delicious and nutritious, and pleasing
I feel passionate about hugging those I love really tight and telling them how much I love them
I feel passionate about spending my day doing those things that bring me extreme joy
I feel passionate about what is in store for me in the future
I feel passionate about the things I want to accomplish
I feel passionate about sharing my passion with others who feel the same way

I love the feeling of passion and the life giving energy that is coursing through me because of it
When I feel the feeling of passion I feel the certainty of all things working out
When I feel the feeling of passion I feel the certainty of giving and receiving love
When I feel the feeling of passion I know that no one can buck my current
When I feel the feeling of passion I know who I really am and what I can accomplish
When I feel the feeling of passion I know I can make things happen
When I feel the feeling of passion I feel everything in the universe yielding to my desires
When I feel the feeling of passion I feel decisive and sure
When I feel the feeling of passion my path seems easy and fun
When I feel the feeling of passion I have clear vision
When I feel the feeling of passion I feel I am on top of the world

I love feeling the feeling of passion
I love knowing that I can feel this way at will

I love knowing that when I follow my bliss I can find passion in every moment of every day
I am ready to live life with passion
I want to be a powerful creator – someone who creates with focus and passion
I love the feeling of joy in my heart that comes with the fast moving energy of passion
Passion is life giving, Passion is addictive, Passion is seductive, Passion is satisfying
Thank you God for an opportunity to live a life full of passion. I love you. I love life.

Word of the day

Celebrate!

www.zmahoon.com

47. Celebrate!

Dear God, thank you for this brand new day
Today I want to celebrate being alive
Life is such a wonderful gift, I want to celebrate it everyday
Today I want to celebrate waking up to blue skies, and bright sunshine
Today I want to celebrate the feeling of wellbeing
Today I want to celebrate peace and relaxation
Today I want to celebrate the abundance that is flowing into my life in so many ways

I have an abundance of good health
I have an abundance of good friends
I have an abundance of love in my life
I have an abundance of peace and joy
I have so much to appreciate and celebrate that I could go on for ever

I celebrate the fact that I can see
I celebrate the fact that I can walk and talk
I celebrate the fact that my children are amazing beings
I celebrate that fact that I live in a beautiful house in a beautiful place
I celebrate the fact that I can go where ever I want to and do whatever pleases me
I celebrate the fact that I can be who I want to be
I celebrate the fact that I am who I want to be and I love it
I love who I am
I celebrate God's love for me
I celebrate that I am perfect in God's eyes
I celebrate that I always have God's light showing me the way forward

My heart fills with joy when I think of all the things I have in my life to celebrate
I want more things to celebrate and be happy about
I understand that the feeling of celebration is just the feeling of heightened appreciation
I know that being in a state of appreciation is just a decision I can make
I can make that decision in every moment of every day
I am making that decision right now in this very moment
Today I will look for things to appreciate and celebrate
I will celebrate big things and small
I will celebrate and appreciate all the people who co-create with me
I will celebrate the journey of life, and appreciate where I am

Where I am today is perfect in every way
Today I will celebrate all the things that have brought me to this perfect place and time
Today I will celebrate where I am going and what I am reaching for
Today I will celebrate that I am here in this brand new day with the zest for life
And when I end this day I will celebrate all the things that have gone well for me
And all the people who have co-created with me
And all the things that are still lined-up for me in the future
Thank you Dear God for this opportunity to celebrate life. I love you. I love life.

Word of the day

Amazing!

www.zmahoon.com

48. Amazing

Dear God, Thank you for another brand new day
I intend to make the most of this amazing day
I intend to appreciate everything and everyone around me
Today I intend to feel with my heart how amazing people are
Like the people who create new gadgets and gizmos
Like the people who are driven to accomplish great feats of agility and strength
Like the people who have kind hearts and helping hands

Today I intent to see with my eyes the amazing wonders of this world
Like the beautifully colored fish in the waters
Like the birds that soar high
Like the amazing beautiful flowers so delicate and so perfect in every way
Like the trees, and the bees and the animals that all add to the diversity and beauty of our planet
Today I intent to hear the sounds of nature
Like the sound of running water
Like the sound of the wind blowing through the leaves
Like the amazingly beautiful music I love to hear each day
Like the sound of children playing and laughing and having a good time

Today I intend to use all my senses to feel my way forward
I intend to consciously define my preferences about what I like
I intend to focus only upon that which feels good
I intend to appreciate, appreciate, appreciate, for there are so many amazing things for me to appreciate
I get it now that this world with its diversity has been created for me
It is for me to choose from

It is for me to enjoy
It is for my pleasure

I love the feeling of amazement that I feel when I see something I have never seen before
I remember how it felt the first time I saw fireworks - I remember how amazing that was
I remember the first time I saw a 3D movie and how amazing that was
I remember the first time I saw whales and how amazing that was
I remember the first time I held my babies and how amazing that was

I love the feeling of amazement that I feel when I hear a story about how wonderful people are
I love the feeling of amazement that I feel when things come together magically, unexpectedly
I love the feeling of amazement, it makes me feel alive
It makes me feel excited about life
It makes me want to look for more amazing things to experience
I want to be one who is easily amazed
I know that the feeling of being amazed is the feeling of utmost appreciation
I want more of that
I want more things to be happy and amazed about
I want to keep living an interesting life day after day after day

A life that is full of amazement and appreciation
A life that is full of love and joy and freedom
A life that is satisfying in every way
Thank you Dear God for giving me the opportunity to allow all good things to come into my life

Today I will bring the attitude of amazement to my day, rather than wait to be amazed
I know that when I can achieve the attitude without waiting for things to change then I have truly mastered the art of living, and that is what I want. Thank you Dear God for your love. I love you. I love life, and I am ready to be amazed.

Word of the day

Love

www.zmahoon.com

49. Love

Dear God, Thank you for this wonderful new day
I love the feeling of feeling love
I love loving; I am the happiest when I love
It doesn't matter to me if I get love from other people because I have the love of God
I know God loves me
I know God loves me because things always work out for me
I know God loves me because I can see the evidence of it in the life I live
I know God loves me exactly the way I am
I know God is always shining a light on me to show me my way

God love is pure and perfect and always flowing
It is the only love I need
When I can feel God's love for me I am in a place of alignment
When I am in a place of alignment I can look at all things and all people with a perspective of love
It feels good to love
It feels good to love because I am love
Because I am love, I must flow love to be me

Today I will flow love to everyone I meet
Today I will see the perfection God sees in all creation
Today I will see the perfection God sees in me
Today I will consciously receive God's love and feel its warmth surround me
Today I will consciously allow myself to flow love

I understand that love does not need reciprocity
In fact, when love needs reciprocity – is it really love?

God's love is unconditional, it flows to me all the time regardless of my behavior

I understand that to be truly at peace and to be truly happy I must flow my love unconditionally

I want to be one who flows love unconditionally to myself and to all those around me

I want to co-create with those who understand unconditional love

I want to co-create with those who understand alignment

I want to co-create with those who know how to tend to their own joy

I want to co-create with those who appreciate creation and love life

I want to co-create with those who are not only a match to who I am today, but those who can keep pace with who I am becoming

I want to co-create because it is more fun to co-create

It is more fun to share a delicious conversation

It is more fun to share appreciation for a beautiful sunset or a starry night

I submit that I must first find perfection in me, in order to find those who will reflect it back to me

Today I want to be kind to myself

Today I want to appreciate myself and love myself for who I am

I am a powerful creator

I love who I am and what I have created

I love my curiosity

I love my ability to learn and grow

I love that I am a good friend

I love that I am an amazing parent

I love that I always do my best

I love that I love people

I love my understanding of my guidance system

I love my ability to use my power of focused thought

I love my talents and what makes me unique

I love me. I am amazing.
I can have be or do anything I want
I am unlimited
I am love
Thank you God for the love in my heart. I love you. I love me. I love creation. I love life.

Word of the day

Potential

www.zmahoon.com

50. Potential

Dear God, Thank you for this wonderful new day full of potential
There is potential for many good things to start making their way to me
There is potential for growth
There is potential for more love
There is potential for better health
There is potential for increased abundance
There is potential for more clarity
There is potential for more joy
There is potential for more of everything I want
I acknowledge that what I want is the feeling of love, the feeling of health, the feeling of abundance and joy and clarity, and how it comes is not important to me – I know that the potential is there

Potential means believing that there is always a way
Potential means believing that things can change
Potential means believing that there is a silver lining around every cloud
Potential means believing that where I am right now is a good place
Potential means that there is good in all my choices
Potential means allowing good things
Potential means receiving good things
Potential means leaving the door open for all good things to surprise me

I love knowing that there is always potential for more
I love knowing that I am full of potential
I am full of the potential to have, be or do anything I want
I am unlimited
I have unlimited potential
All things are possible for me
I love knowing that every person I meet is full of potential to achieve

I love knowing that every situation has positive potential
I love knowing that potential is like a little spark and all I have to do is to allow it to grow into a flame

The feeling of potential is the feeling of hope
The feeling of potential is the feeling of knowing that all I have to do is to have faith
The feeling of potential is the feeling of looking and finding something to appreciate in every one and every thing
The feeling of potential is the feeling of being open
It is the feeling of allowing all people, things and events to rise to their maximum potential

I love knowing that there is potential in everything
I love knowing that my potential is always calling me towards my growth and my greater wellbeing
I love knowing that I will forever be discovering more potential in myself and others around me and in all situations and events
I love knowing that I create my own potential
I create the potential for everything that comes to me
Today I will think thoughts of appreciation and keep the door to positive potential open
Today I will treat every person and every event in my life with the perspective of believing in unseen potential

I know that I do not have to see the potential for it to be there – I just have to believe that it is there and it is
I know that You Dear God always believe in my potential
And today I commit to believing in my own potential and my ability to create anything
I love the feeling of potential

Thank you Dear God for the understanding that you have blessed me with.
Thank you for showing me my own potential to have, be or do anything I want.
I love you. I love life.

Word of the day

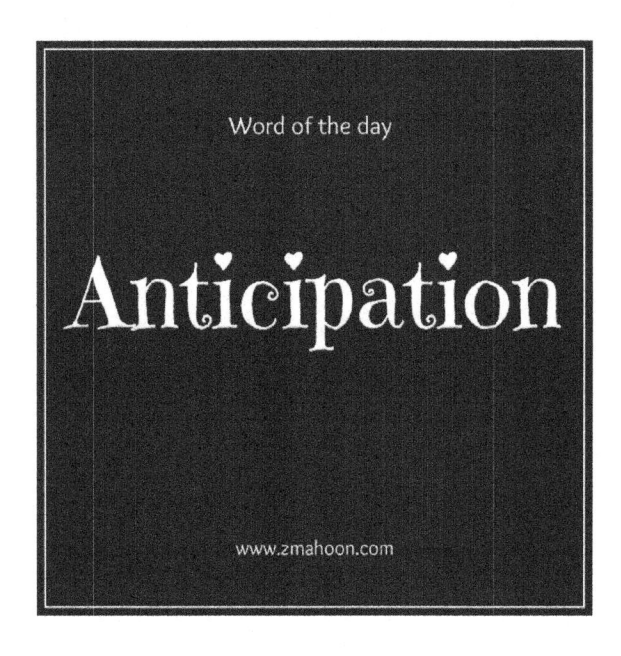

Anticipation

www.zmahoon.com

51. Anticipation

Dear God, Thank you for this brand new day – a day of anticipation
I love the life giving feeling of anticipation, something to look forward to
I understand that that is what life's journey is all about: looking forward; positive anticipation
I understand that negative emotion means that I am anticipating that which I do not want
And positive emotion means that I am anticipating that which will make me happy when it arrives

I want to be one who is always anticipating positively
I want to anticipate good things coming to me all the time
I want to anticipate a future full of joy
I want to anticipate a perfect unfolding for each day
I want to anticipate meeting wonderful people, and going to new places
I want to anticipate abundance and prosperity
I want to anticipate perfect health and agility
I want to anticipate being surrounded by love

I can anticipate all good things coming to me, because I believe that they are
I understand that positive anticipation is a reflection of my beliefs
Anticipation means that I believe that things are always working out for me
Not only that, I believe that things are always working out better than I anticipate
Not only that, I believe that many good things are coming my way that I could not even begin to anticipate
Not only that, I believe that You Dear God have the power to yield to me more than I could ever logically anticipate

Not only that, I believe that I can anticipate all things being possible, and that as long as I can hold that door of positive anticipation open You have the power to squeeze through that crack many miracles
Today I choose positive anticipation

I love feeling the feeling of positive anticipation
It feels like the moment before a plane touches down
It feels like the moment before I see a long awaited friend
It feels like the moment before digging into a delicious meal
It feels like the moment before the music reaches a crescendo
It feels like coming over a hill and feasting over a beautiful panorama
It feels like the moment before an orgasm
It feels like powerful energy on its way to manifestation

I love that feeling of knowing that my desire is about to manifest
It is a place of sureness and joy – a place of anticipation
I love feeling the joy of positive anticipation Dear God
Thank you for all the opportunities I have had in the past to feel the powerful feeling of anticipation
I love feeling the feeling of anticipation where I stand today
I love knowing that life is a process of discovery, a process of reaching for more
I love knowing that there will always be more wonderful things to anticipate and look forward to
Thank you for the love you send my way every day
Thank you for the guidance I know is always there for me
Thank you for this brand new day and the life giving feeling of anticipation it brings with it
I love you Dear God. I love life. I love the feeling of anticipation.

Word of the day

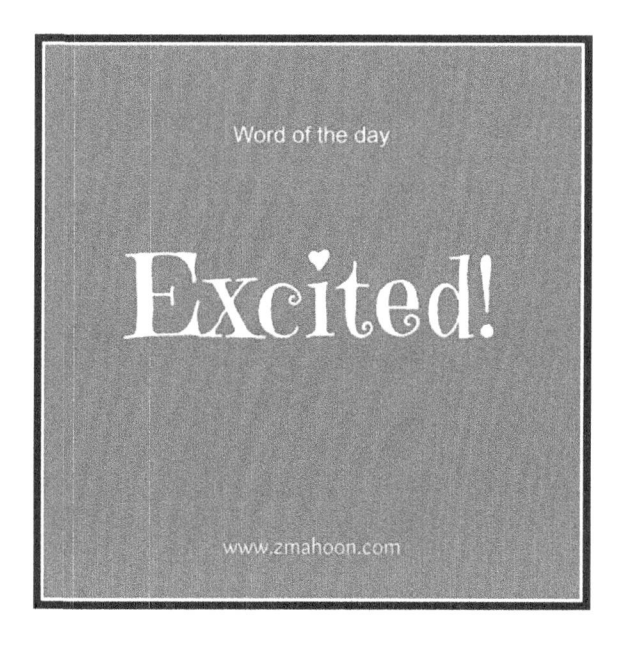

Excited!

www.zmahoon.com

52. Excited!

Dear God, Thank you for this exciting new day!
I am looking forward to the perfect unfolding of this beautiful day
I have slept well and awakened refreshed, feeling happy and relaxed
I am appreciating the luxury of just being in this momentum cradled comfortably in my bed
I am loving the quietness of the world around me and the peace within me
This is going to be a very good day
Today I am deliberately looking for things to be excited about
Today I want to be like a child creating opportunities for excitement, just because it's fun

To skip when I could walk
To laugh just because
To sing a song out loud
To stomp in the puddles
To dance around in circles
To explore and shout
To play with an empty box
To catch a dogs tail
To run to the door when the bell rings
To bounce a ball
To open a present
To bang on the pots and pans – Oh! What fun!
These are the things excitement is made of

I can be excited and happy all the time, because I remember, I remember how to be happy
I remember that there is excitement to be extracted from every day

Each day is about play, each day is about love, each day is about joy, each day is about excitement
I am going to don the attitude of excitement today
I am going to be excited about the food I eat
I am going to be excited about the people I meet
I am going to be excited about the work I do
I love the feeling of excitement
I love the feeling of thriving and moving forward
I love being in love with life and feeling excited about everything

I can close my eyes and connect with the feeling of excitement at any time I want
I know that the more I connect with the feeling of excitement the better I feel
I know that connecting with the feeling of excitement brings me more excitement
I like feeling excited about my life and about the joy in the lives of the people around me
I like feeling excited about people winning lotteries and accomplishing great success
I like feeling excited about envisioning my children's accomplishments
I like feeling excited about creating consciously and knowing that when I create it is done

It is done, it is done, it is done
I can feel that it is done
I love the thrill bumps that I feel from the excitement of knowing that it is done
And now all I have to do is to relax and let it in

Thank you God for the feeling of excitement. I love feeling excited and I ask for your help in reminding me that I can find excitement in the smallest of things. Thank you Dear God. I love you. I love life. I love excitement.

Word of the day

Accomplish

www.zmahoon.com

53. Accomplish

Dear God, what a wonderful day to wake up to
A day to accomplish many things
Thank you for this opportunity
Today I want to focus on just this one day and make the most of it
I want to accomplish control over my thoughts and prayers
I want to accomplish joy
Joy comes from appreciation
Today I want to find things to appreciate
Today I want to accomplish alignment with the way God thinks
Today I want to think my thoughts in a manner that open the door to receiving what is already given
Thank you Dear God for an opportunity to accomplish all this

I love and appreciate the blue sky this morning
I love and appreciate the golden sunshine
I love and appreciate the big beautiful trees in my backyard
I love and appreciate the warm glow covering my heart
I love and appreciate my cats and their purring in appreciation
I love and appreciate my dog's zest for life
I love and appreciate the feeling of energy flowing when I write
I love and appreciate that all is well in this moment
This moment is perfect in every way

I love and appreciate my children and their hugs and the love and warmth I feel for them
And I want more of that
I love and appreciate the good times we share, the laughter and the joy
And I want more of that
I love and appreciate my capacity to learn and grow

And I want more of that
I love and appreciate that I am always reaching for more
And I want more of that
I love and appreciate my ability to teach
And I want more of that
I love and appreciate the stability of my world
And I want more of that
I love and appreciate my ability to meet all my commitments
And I want more of that
I love and appreciate my capacity for enjoying my work
And I want more of that
I love and appreciate all my friends
And I want more of that
I love and appreciate the feeling of love and appreciation
And I want more of that

I know that feeling that feeling is all I need to accomplish
For when I can do that I am in alignment with my Source
And that is all I need to accomplish in order for all things to come to me
I am happy and eager about the ways in which my path will unfold and surprise me
I know now that all I need to accomplish is unconditional joy
Thank you God for all the joy in my life
I love you. I love life.

Word of the day

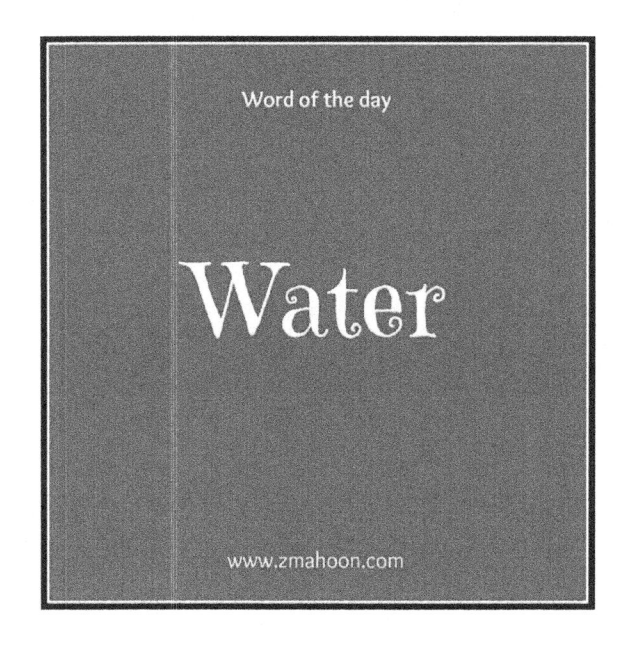

Water

www.zmahoon.com

54. Water

Dear God thank you for creating water
I love a refreshing drink of water
Drinking water makes me feel alive and fresh
Drinking water helps my physical body to maintain it's balance
I love drinking water
I love how water helps to clean things
I love how clean the trees look after a rain, their colours look brighter than ever

I love all the beverages we make with water
I love immersing myself in water and feeling light
I love sitting by a running steam or a lake and watching how water flows
I love the sound of running water
I love the sound of waves crashing on the beach
I love and appreciate the life giving nature of water
The Earth thrives because of water
We grow crops because of water
I love water
I love all the things I have learnt from water
I've learnt that water always finds a way to keep going
It doesn't matter if there are obstacles along the way, water always finds a way around them
Water keeps moving towards its destination
Sometimes it moves slowly and sometimes it moves fast, but it is always moving

When a rock shows up in its path water doesn't stop to worry
Water always finds a way
Water always reflects my emotion back to me

When I am happy, it seems bright and alive and happy
When I am sad, it seems gloomy
It reminds me that the whole world is like that reflecting back to me what I am feeling and therefore creating
Water reminds me that there is abundance in the world
Water reminds me that there is balance in the world and that nature knows what it is doing

Water reminds me that clarity is beautiful and that it is inevitable
Water reminds me that there are always new places to go to and new things to do
Thank you water for your contribution in helping me understand the creative process
Thank you water for refreshing me and energizing me every day
Thank you for always being there for me as a reminder of how things work
I love you. I love life.

Word of the day

Fun!

www.zmahoon.com

55. Fun!

Dear God, thank you for another beautiful day – a day full of fun
I am understanding that life is all about having fun, and a new day is a new opportunity for that
I know that appreciating the fun I've had is a way for creating more fun in the future
I know that anticipating more fun in the future gives me creative control over my life
I can extract fun from so many things
I have fun enjoying good food, the pleasure of tasting is one of the most amazing things in life
I have fun enjoying a relaxed drive in the summer with the windows open and the breeze blowing in my face
I have fun, Oh so much fun, feasting my eyes on fall colors – I absolutely love and adore the fiery reds and the oranges and yellows
I have fun going for a long walk along the creek, listening to the water as it gushes forward

I have fun spotting fish in the water
I have fun sitting in meditation on a log with the sun warming my back
I have fun when my children tackle me down and climb all over me for hugs
I have fun when I laugh so hard that I have tears streaming down my face
I have fun when my cat sits on my lap and purrs loudly in appreciation
I have fun when I go shopping and find many things I want on sale
I have fun when I go for a swim and let the water cradle me as I float
I have fun when I have a good discussion with a friend
I have fun when I hear children playing happily outside
There is so much fun to be had in everyday and I want more of that
I want to have fun visiting new places and exploring the world
I want to have fun making new friends and learning new things

I want to have fun watching my children grow and be happy
I want to have fun writing new books and doing more talks and workshops
I want to have fun riding a bike through beautiful trails with the breeze in my face

I want to have fun doing what I like to do, being who I want to be
I want to find new ways to have fun
I love the fun I have when I share my fun with others
Today I want to focus on everything from perspective of extracting the most fun
I love the feeling of fun
I love the feeling of knowing that more fun things are on their way
Thank you God for giving me so many fun things to enjoy. I love and appreciate them all, and I want more of them. I love you. I love life.

Word of the day

Freedom

www.zmahoon.com

56. Freedom

Dear God, thank you for this wonderful new day
I love waking up feeling relaxed and happy and free
I understand that freedom is the natural way of all beings
All things in nature thrive because they are free
I look at the birds and appreciate the feeling of freedom they must feel when they fly – I can close my eyes and feel the freedom of being a bird and looking down on the world

I look at the trees and appreciate the feeling of freedom they must feel as they reach for the sky – I can feel that freedom just throwing my arms up and reaching for the sun
I look at squirrels in my backyard and appreciate the feeling of freedom they must feel as they swing from tree to tree, and I can close my eyes and feel the exhilaration and freedom of that
I look at the clouds floating by and appreciate the feeling of freedom I would feel if I were a cloud, floating happily
I can close my eyes and feel the feeling of freedom I would feel if I were a fish, swimming wherever I wish

I can feel my own freedom in the movement of my body as I run
I can feel my own freedom when I feel the breeze on my face
I can feel the feeling of freedom when I gaze at open fields
I can feel the feeling f freedom as I look upon the expanse of water in the lakes
I love feeling the feeling of freedom
Today I want to feel the feeling of freedom in everything I do and everywhere I go
I want to be free
I want to be free to do whatever pleases me

Free to be who I want to be
Free to say what I want to say
Free to think what I want to think
Free to feel how I want to feel
Free to enjoy the things that mean the most to me
Free to make my own choices
Free to love, free to laugh, free to sing and dance
Freedom is what I want
I was born to be free

Dear God, please show me the path to more freedom
I want more freedom of time to do all the things I want to do
I want more freedom of time to have fun
I want more freedom of money, money flowing in and money flowing out with ease
I want to feel free to spend money, give money, and multiply money
I want to feel free to enjoy travelling all over the world
I want to feel free to buy beautiful things and bring them home
I want to feel free to help others find their freedom
Thank you God for all the freedom I already have in my life and I want more of that
I love and appreciate those who have created freedom for themselves
I love and appreciate those who have freedom of time
I love and appreciate all those who have freedom of money
I love and appreciate all those who have physical freedom, and healthy bodies

I love and appreciate all those who are showing me examples of how they created freedom
And I acknowledge that I want that too

I want more freedom Dear God and I am feeling blessed because I know all things are possible
The freedom that I want is not only possible, it is probable,
It is not only probable it is certain – it is done, it is done, it is done, it is done
I love you Dear God, I love life, I love freedom. Freedom to have, be or do anything I want. Life is good!

Word of the day

Nice

www.zmahoon.com

57. Nice

Dear God, thank you for another brand new day
It's nice to wake up to sunshine and clear blue skies
It's nice to feel relaxed and happy
It's nice to feel the health of my physical body
It's nice to hold my warm mug of coffee and sip it slowly, savoring every drop

It's nice to look outside and feast my eyes on the beautiful world
It's nice to look forward to a day that is bound to be satisfying
It's nice to wake up appreciating all the things that are working for me
I love the wellbeing that surrounds me each day
It's nice to feel good
It's nice to know that things are always working out for me
It's nice to know that I can start from where ever I am and change my future, making it better
It's nice to know that I have power, I have power over my life
It's nice to know that I can have, be or do anything I want
It's nice to know that the simple act of appreciation is what brings me things I want
It's nice to know that I can train myself to appreciate, appreciation is easy
It's nice to know that all is well in my world

Thank you for all the nice people in my life – those I work with, those I help, those I love, those who love me
Thank you for all the nice things I own, my beautiful house, my car, my laptop, my cell phone and so much more
Thank you for all the nice places I've been to and the beauty I have seen
Thank you for all the knowledge I have gained about the way things work

Thank you for the peace in my heart and the feeling of satisfaction I feel everyday
I love my life, I love me

Wouldn't it be nice if I could have more freedom of time?
Wouldn't it be nice if I could have more freedom of money?
Wouldn't it be nice if I could manifest a loving relationship?
Wouldn't it be nice if....

It is nice to know that You know what I want and that it is already lined up for me
It is nice to know that all I have to do is to have fun every day, appreciate a lot, laugh a lot, relax a lot and let You bring me all the things I want
It is very nice to know that I can be like a tree, firmly rooted in my faith, knowing that all things I need will come to me
It is very nice to know that I can be like a tree, knowing, loving, giving, and letting You have your way with me
It is very nice to know that I can be like a tree allowing the seasons to change and enjoying each of them
It is very nice to know that I can be like a tree, standing in appreciation of all of the world around me
It is very nice to know that I can be like a tree, growing every day, reaching for the sky
It is very nice to know that I can be like a tree, contributing to the wellness and beauty of the world
Thank you God for this wonderful new day. Today I feel happy where I am and eager for more.

Word of the day

Thankful

www.zmahoon.com

58. Thankful

Dear God, I am so thankful for this beautiful new day
Thank you for another opportunity to enjoy time with my children and the people I love

Thank you for the sun that shines
Thank you for the birds that sing
Thank you for the beautiful trees
Thank you for the magnificent mountains
Thank you for the streams and rivers
Thank you for the food we eat
Thank you for the love that flows
Thank you for the joy we share
Thank you God for everything

There is so much in my life to be thankful for
I am thankful for the journey that has made me who I am
I love who I am
I am thankful for the people that I have met along the way, those who have instigated my growth and those who have helped me along
I am thankful for the opportunities that have come my way
I have led a truly wonderful life

I am thankful for all the beautiful places I have experienced and the things I have seen
I am thankful for my beautiful mother and all the things I learnt from her
I am thankful for my amazing father who taught me about unconditional love
I am thankful for my wonderful children who always give me love and joy
I am thankful for my friends who are always there for me when I reach out

I am thankful for the love that surrounds me and flows from me
I am thankful for the powerful teachers from whom I've had the opportunity to learn
I am thankful for the work I do to help others along on their journeys
I am thankful for all those who help me to earn a living
I am thankful for the prosperity that flows into my life
I am thankful for my health and my stamina and wellbeing
I am thankful for the knowing I feel in my heart
I am thankful for the peace I feel inside me

There is so much to be thankful for Dear God
Thank you for the love you are always sending my way
Thank you for the guidance that I know is always there
Thank you for making me the object of your attention
Thank you for showing me that all things are possible
Thank you for allowing me the freedom to choose
Thank you for helping me figure how law of attraction works
Thank you for helping me see that we are all the same, we have the same hopes and dreams
Thank you for helping me understand the value of my guidance system and how it works
Thank you making this world so full of diversity from which I can express my preferences
Thank you, thank you, thank you
Thank you for all my treasures
I love you, I love life.

Word of the day

Easy!

www.zmahoon.com

59. Easy

Dear God, Thank you for this wonderful new day
I love waking up to the feeling of ease and relaxation
It feels good to just curl up and soak up the warmth of my bed
It feels good to stretch and feel the wellbeing of my body as I prepare to step into the world
I love the feeling of ease and flow in all things
I love the ease with which water flows as I shower
I love feeling the contrast of hot and cold water
I love the refreshing feeling of water streaming all over me
I love how water always flows towards the path of least resistance

Water always finds the easiest way
Water always keeps flowing
I want to be like water, always looking for and finding the easy way
I love the ease and flow in the cycle of nature
Trees don't strain to grow, birds don't strain as they look for food
Seasons don't strain to change – there is ease and flow in everything
Trees don't fight with each other as they reach for sunshine, they all find a way to the sun
The sun rises easily every day
Geese don't strain their necks with worry

Everything in nature is easy because everything in nature is letting You have Your way
Nature is always showing me that when I trust life is easy
I appreciate that, and I want more of that in my life – I want more trust, I want more ease
I want to always look for and find the easy way, the path of most joy

I love it when I find ease and flow on the road, always going at the right speed in the right lane
I love it when I find ease and flow at work, co-creating with happy appreciative people
I love it when I find ease and flow at home, getting everything done in perfect timing
I love the ease and flow I feel when I write and share my views
I love the ease and flow with which money comes into my life
I love the ease and flow and fun with which I spend money, knowing that there is always more coming
I love the ease and flow of my physical body, my stamina and my agility
I love the ease and flow of words as they flow from me when I do these rampages
I love the ease with which I flow love to all those around me
I love the ease with which things flow into my life and I want more of that
I love how the easier it gets the easier it gets
I love feeling easy and relaxed about life
I love life

I am beginning to see the power of positive momentum in my life and I want more of that
I love knowing that "ease" is just an attitude, a way of thinking and feeling that I have complete control over
I love knowing that I can feel easy whenever I want to
I love knowing that I can tell the difference between when I am feeling easy and not
I love knowing that I know what to do to feel easy
I love knowing that feeling easy is about turning my attention to things that make me happy
I love knowing that when I surrender to You and let You do my work life is easy

Please help me remember Dear God that I have you with me at all times and that all things are possible
Please help me remember that all things are easy because You make them easy
I want all good things to flow to me easily
I want to laugh easily
I want to love a lot
I want to feel the ease and comfort that nature feels in all things
I love the path of ease and flow and the joy that comes with trusting that all is always well
I love knowing that I can adopt a perspective of ease consciously and when I do good things happen
Thank you God for showing me the path of trust, the path of joy, the path of ease
I love you. I love life. I love being easy about all things.

Word of the day

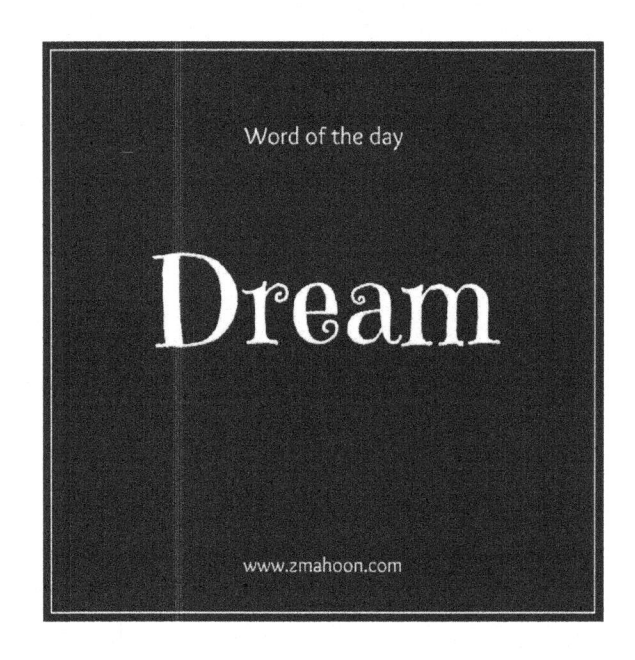

Dream

www.zmahoon.com

60. Dream

Dear God, thank you for this beautiful brand new day
I feel excited as I step into consciousness from my dreams
Whatever those dreams where have left me feeling happy and refreshed
I like this feeling, I like that it is telling me that all is well in my world
I like that I can start a new day with a new perspective on my hopes and dreams

I am learning that it's ok to dream big
In fact, it is fun to think big
I am learning that the purpose of dreaming is just to dream
I am learning that dreaming is just a game that is supposed to be fun
I am learning that I don't have to work on any of my dreams to make them come true
I am learning that dreams are just another place for me to go to have fun
I am learning that I don't need to tell You the difference between things I really want and things that are just fun to think about and dream about

I enjoy the creative process of dreaming – I enjoy day dreaming and conscious creating
I enjoy dreaming about going to far away lands with amazing landscapes
I enjoy dreaming about open seas and starry nights, fields full of flowers and blue skies
I enjoy dreaming about flying like a bird, and swinging on a rope, swimming like a mermaid and exploring unseen places
I enjoy dreaming about creating wealth and prosperity
I enjoy dreaming about having a loving relationship to share my appreciation of life with
I enjoy dreaming about my children and their accomplishments

I love the feeling of freedom I feel when I dream
I love the feeling of unlimited possibilities in a dream
I love that I can create many versions of my dreams
I love knowing that the process of dreaming helps me to clarify my preferences
I love knowing that I can reach anyone I want through my dreams
I love that I can be whoever I want to be in my dreams
I love that I can create a vivid reality in my dreams

I am beginning to see how the process of dreaming helps me to understand conscious creating
I am beginning to appreciate my ability to focus with intensity
I love dreaming about a joyous future for myself and my family
I love dreaming about having, and doing anything I want
I love dreaming about the wellbeing of the planet, seeing this world as a place of peace and joy
I love dreaming about abundance and prosperity for all, a world where everyone feels fulfilled
I love dreaming about happy faces and beautiful places
I love dreaming about creativity and progress
I love knowing that everything in this world was once a dream
I love knowing that this world was once a dream
I love knowing that dreaming is an important part of life
I love hearing about the hopes and dreams of others
I love the warm feeling I feel in my heart when I hear the stories people tell about their dreams coming true

I want to dream more dreams and hear more stories of dreams come true
I want to tell my own stories of my dreams come true
Today I want to dream some more – create some more
Thank you God for this gift of creativity. I love you. I love life.

Word of the day

New

www.zmahoon.com

61. New

Dear God, thank you for this wonderful new day
A new beginning, an opportunity to look at things differently
I submit that when I look at things differently, the things I look at seem different

Today, I want to look at things with a fresh new, positive feeling perspective
Today, I want to look at the world as if it were brand new
Today I want to be curious and inviting
Today I want to open and trusting
Today I want to thrill in the moment and be happy

I remember the feeling of new things and new adventures
I remember what it fun it was to go shopping for new school supplies
I remember the fun of new clothes and new shoes
I remember the fun of new places to visit
I remember the fun of unwrapping presents
I remember the fun of blowing bubbles and playing with balloons
I remember the fun I had the first time I saw fireworks and the first time I was on a roller coaster

I love new experiences and new things to try – I want more of that
I love how I can rearrange my furniture to make my home feel new
I love bringing new things home and making my living spaces feel fresh and happy
I love finding new recipes and cooking new things for my friends and family to enjoy
I love making new friends and getting to know people and help them with their hopes and dreams

I love the birthing of a new book or a new idea to write an article
I love dreaming new dreams about things I want to do, places I want to visit, and the life I want to live

It is fun to find more new things to enjoy
It is fun to look forward to something new and different
There are so many new things in my life everyday – for nothing stays the same
There are new clouds in the sky, and soon there will be new leaves and new flowers all around
I love watching and feeling the Earth wake up to a new spring each year
I love the shiny new leaves sprouting from the trees and the new furry and feathered visitors in my backyard
I love knowing that every day I wake up as a new me
I love knowing that every day I have an opportunity to feel and think differently
I love knowing that there will always be new things to want, new ways to feel
I love knowing that I can always find a new way to focus my thoughts
I love knowing that the Universe is always conspiring to bring me something new

I like the fresh invigorating feeling of new beginnings, new desires, new plans
I love dreaming new dreams
Thank you God for continuously sending me new things to appreciate
I want a constant flow of new things, people and experiences that bring me joy
I love you God. I love my life and the new opportunities it brings me. I love me.

Word of the day

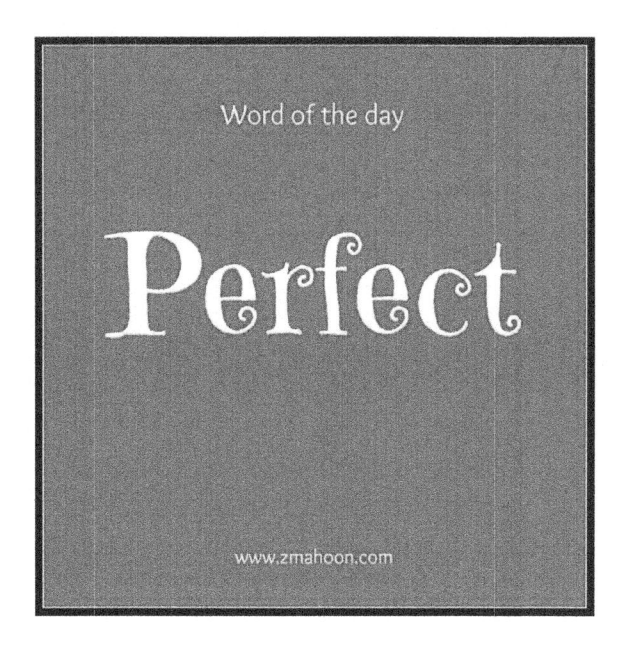

Perfect

www.zmahoon.com

62. Perfect

Dear God, Thank you for this perfect new day
I love waking up to a perfect sunrise
I love feeling the perfect peace and quiet of my house
I love my perfect morning coffee
I love the perfection of the world around me
I love the perfection of the flowers, their colors, their shapes, and their sizes
I love the perfection of the trees, the perfection of their branches and their leaves
I love the perfectly blue skies with puffy white clouds floating gently by

There is so much for us to appreciate all around us
Thank you for giving us so many wonderful opportunities to appreciate
I love knowing that all I need to do is to keep the momentum of appreciation going to make my day perfect
I love knowing that each perfect day makes for a perfect life
I can see the perfection of the contrast in my life
I can see that contrast helps me to clarify my desires to a perfection
I know now that I am always at the perfect place at the perfect time
I know now that the Universe has a perfect system for matching up things, people and events
I know now that there is perfection in everything
I know that all creations are perfect

Perfection feels like the love I feel when I look at my children
Perfection feels like the smiles I see on the people that I meet
Perfection feels like the curiosity of a baby
Perfection feels like the perfect timing of a joke that makes me laugh
Perfection feels like the feeling of knowing where to find things and what to do with them

Perfection feels like the warmth in my home as I share a meal with family and friends
Perfection feels like the warmth of my cat as she purrs away beside me
Perfection feels like the love I feel when I am in deep meditation
Perfection feels like the feeling of freedom I feel when I gaze on open waters with the breeze blowing on my face
Perfection feels like a beautiful yellow butter cup shining in the sunlight
Perfection feels like meeting a good friend and feeling the joy of connection
Perfection feels like the moment when I can see the absolute synchronicity of the thoughts I think and the things I create
Perfection feels like the glow I feel inside me when my heart seems to expand with love and joy

I love the feeling of perfection
My life is perfect in so many ways
Thank you God for all my blessings
Today I want to feel the perfection of the love you feel for me
Today I want to find ways to appreciate the perfection of all my blessings
Today I want my journey on life's path to unfold with perfect ease
Today I want to feel the perfection of my own being
Today I want to look at the people I meet and see the perfection of their beings
Today I want to know in my heart that all things are perfect exactly the way they are
Thank you Dear God for creating perfect balance in the Universe. I love you. I love life.

Word of the day

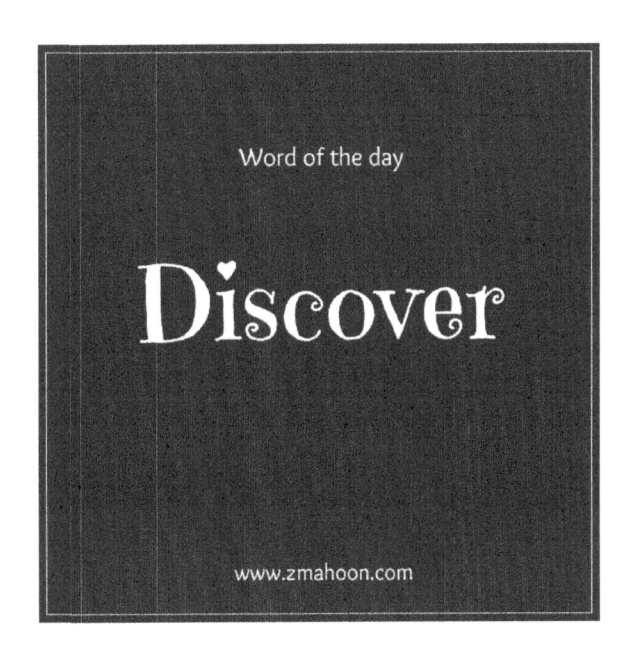

Discover

www.zmahoon.com

63. Discover

Dear God, thank you for this wonderful new day
I am looking forward to a day full of exciting discoveries
I love discovering new things
I love the process of discovery
I love asking questions and discovering the answers
I love surprises that bring me to new discoveries I had never thought about
I love the feeling of knowing when an inspired thought brings me to a new place of discovery
I love knowing that there is so much more yet to be discovered
I love knowing that nature and the universe are always conspiring to create new things for us to discover
New species of living things waiting to be discovered, new plants and flowers, and bugs and beetles, butterflies and moths
New places on Earth and beyond

I love the genius and creativity of those who focus on discovering new ways of doing things
I love knowing that new discoveries will always keep coming and the world will constantly keep changing and growing
I want to discover new things about nature
I want to discover interesting new ideas
I want to discover more about my own talents and capabilities
I want to discover more about my own power to create and manifest
I want to discover more about my ability to think on purpose
I want to discover more ways to be joyful and appreciate
I want to discover more ways of expressing my love for people, nature and things
I want to discover more about being in the receptive mode, always receiving wellbeing

I want to discover more ways to relax and have fun
I want to discover more ways to allow abundance and prosperity
I want to discover the strength, beauty and health of my physical body
I want to discover the joy of co-creation with others
I want to enjoy the satisfaction of discovery

Thank you God, for always helping me discover my path
Thank you for helping me discover peace within
Thank you for helping me towards love and joy
Thank you for always being there for me in every moment

Today I want to discover joy in little things, like the purring of my cat, and the singing of the birds
Today I want to discover more joy in co-creating with others
Today I want to help others discover their path and their joy
Today I want to be good to myself and others
Today I want you to guide me towards the discovery of that which will bring me joy
Today I want you to guide me towards the discovery of the easy path to things I want
Thank you God for always helping me along. I love you. I love life.

Word of the day

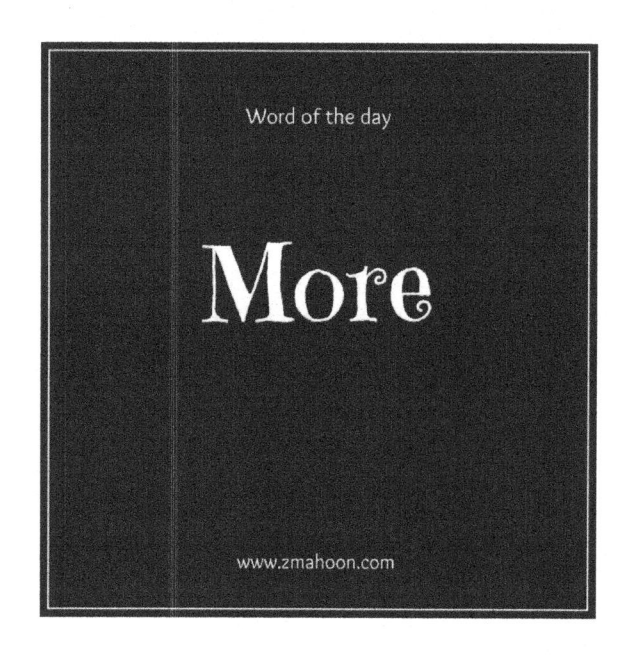

More

www.zmahoon.com

64.　More

Dear God, Thank you for this brand new day, an opportunity to do more, be more, and have more
Abraham says that "more" is the mantra of the Universe
More love, more joy, more abundance, more prosperity, more health
More, more, more, more

There is always more of everything, I like knowing that
I like knowing that when I ask it is always given
I like knowing that all I have to do is to get on to a rampage like this for more to come
I see evidence of more all around me
There is always more air to breathe, more food to eat, more flavors to taste
There is always something more to want, something more to look forward to, something more to love
More places to visit, more things to see, more music to hear, more laughter and jokes to enjoy
More books to read, more people to meet, more love to give and receive
Thank you for this wonderful life where there are always possibilities for more

I love knowing that I am the creator and I can always create more of anything I want with my thought
I can create more love in my life
I can create more prosperity, and more health
I want more
I want more joy
I want more love
I want more prosperity
I want more clarity

I want more nice things to enjoy
I want more satisfying experiences
I want more experiences that make me feel alive
I want more co-creators who make life delicious
I want more confidence
I want more knowledge
I want more evidence of my wellbeing

Today I want to see more evidence of my wellbeing
Today I want to see more evidence of the power of my own thought
Today I want to feel more joy in my heart as I go forward
I want more exciting ideas to flow into my mind
I want more ease and flow in everything I do, everywhere I go and everyone I meet
I want more doors to open for me
I want more things that I have been wanting to make their way into my life with ease and joy
Today I want to feel more alive in every moment
Today I want to pay more attention to the guidance that is always coming my way
Today I want more of all things that are good for me
Dear God, Thank you for this day that is surely bringing me more of all that is good for me. I love you. I love life.

Word of the day

Alright

www.zmahoon.com

65. Alright

Dear God thank you for another brilliant, beautiful day
Everything in my world seems alright today
I feel calm and at peace... whatever will be will be
My thinking about it, worrying about won't help
And I know that there is no sense in that
Because I have learnt that good things happen when I feel good
My feelings always indicate to me the direction of my future manifestation
When I feel good I know I am looking at things the way God wants me to look at them
When I feel bad I know that I am looking at things in a manner that does not serve me
I understand my guidance now
I understand that when I don't feel good I am not ready for the action I am thinking about
I know that I can make myself ready by thinking thoughts of appreciation
I know that regardless of what I think or do
Things always turn out alright

It serves me to believe that things are always working out for me
It serves me to believe that I have help and guidance every step of the way
It serves me to believe that all things are possible
It serves me to believe that I don't need to figure things out
It serves me to believe that God's way is always the best
It serves me to believe that there is always a way whether I can see it or not
It serves me to believe that I can always trust in God's power
It serves me to believe that all is well at all times
It serves me to believe that decisions are easy because no matter what I choose God can lead me to what is best for me
It serves me to believe that I can always find a thought that feels better

And really that is my only work, to always reach for a thought that feels just a little bit better
All is well in my world Dear God
I know and I believe that I will always be alright
In fact, I know and I believe that I can always thrive
I know and I believe that life is good
People are good
Everything that shows up on my path is good for me
I know and I believe that I can always find my way
I know and I believe that anything is possible because it does not depend upon me
I love my life
I love where I have been, where I am today and where I am going
Life is better than alright, life is good
Thank you Dear God for everything I have
I love you. I love life.

Word of the day

Magic!

www.zmahoon.com

66. Magic

Dear God, thank you for this brand new day
Today I want to see magic and wonder in the world around me
I want to see how the magic unfolds, the magic of life
There is magic in the rising sun and the perfection with which it takes its place in the sky
There is magic in the sounds of the birds and the whispering of the breeze
There is magic in the beautiful puffy snowflakes as they stream past the light from the street lamp

I love looking out at the silent world and watching it wake up as if by magic – everything changing in just a few minutes
I love the magic of a mug full of coffee; I love how it feels to hold that warm mug in my hands as I look out on to the trees watching the sun rise
I love the magic of nature and all the wonderful things in creation
I love the magic of life
I love the magic of my body working perfectly, it is amazing how many things it does all on it's own
I love the magic of sight, translating vibration into pictures for me to enjoy the colors and shapes, providing me with endless opportunities to appreciate the beauty of the world around me
I love the magic of sound in music, the sounds of the birds and the world around me
I love the magic of music, so many different beats and lyrics to enjoy
I love the magic of touch and feel, I love how the sun warms the Earth and the magic of sunshine raising spirits and making the world brilliant and beautiful
I love the magic of love, I can feel the vibration of love, its warmth and its joy
I love how the magic of thought brings me things I think about

I love how people call me magically all because I was thinking about them
I love how things fall into my lap by magic all because I wanted them
I love how I can control the magic of thought and more work I do the better it gets
I love the magical feeling of floating because I know all is well in my world
I love the magical feeling of knowing that I have guidance and that my path is continuously unfolding before me
I love the magical feeling of peace in my heart, always happy where I am
I love the magical feeling of elation when something wonderfully unexpected happens
I love the magical feeling of appreciation that I feel when I thank you God for the ease with which my life is yielding me many joys
I love the magical feeling of love that I feel just because it feels good to be in love with life

I love the magic of knowing that I am the creator of my world, that I create the magic in every moment of my life
Thank you for the magic in my life. Thank you for showing me how to create magic, how to enjoy magic, how to share magic, how to make this world a better place
Thank you God for giving me the power to yield magic. I love my magic, I love my life. I love me.

Word of the day

Ready

www.zmahoon.com

67. Ready

Dear God, thank you for this beautiful brand new day
I feel ready to make the best of this day
I feel ready to enjoy every moment from waking up to going to bed
I feel ready to be happy
I feel ready to feel the energy of life around me and inside me
I feel ready to appreciate all the wonderful things I can see
I can see that the world is ready for me to enjoy
I can see that everything is always in the perfect place at the perfect time
I feel ready to explore new things today
I feel ready to receive abundance, freely flowing into my life
I feel ready to receive love and give love
I feel ready to feel the stamina and energy and the health of my physical body

I feel ready to appreciate myself and all the work I've done
I feel ready to appreciate who I am and who I am becoming
I feel ready to appreciate all those who have instigated my growth
I feel ready to appreciate the path that has helped me to the knowing that I now have
I feel ready to go with the ease and flow of life
I feel ready to take the path of least resistance
I feel ready to trust and allow You to Guide me to my wellbeing
I am ready, I am ready, I am ready, I am ready
I am ready for all good things to flow to me easily
I am ready for excitement and eagerness
I am ready for new experiences, places to see, people to meet, things to do
I am ready for a loving relationship that is perfect for me in every way
I am ready for prosperity and abundance beyond measure
I am ready for the joy of feeling sand between my toes

I am ready to feel warmth of the sun warming my back
I am ready to feel the breeze in my face
I am ready for freedom and growth and joy
Thank you Dear God for this wonderful feeling of readiness
I am ready to receive your love and the wonderful things you have lined up for me
I love you. I love life.

Word of the day

Wonder

www.zmahoon.com

68. Wonder

Dear God thank you for this brand new day
Today I want to see the world with the wonder of a child's eye - as if it is brand new and I am brand new too, with brand new eyes and a brand new appreciation!
I know there is wonder in most everything I see
There is wonder in the sun rise and the sunset
There is wonder in the beauty of all the colors of this beautiful planet
There is wonder in the beauty of flowers, and birds and fish – I am always amazed at their colors
There is wonder in the way everything in nature is connected – only you could manage it all Dear God

I wonder how you created the Earth
I wonder how you created the Universe
I wonder how you created so many life forms, animals, birds, plants, and micro-organisms
I wonder how you created the systems that make the world function so smoothly – gravity, the elements, earth, wind, and fire
I wonder how you created the human body with its intricate organs
I wonder how my eyes can see
I wonder how my body can function without my conscious involvement
I wonder at the speed at which my brain processes information
I wonder at the beautiful things people create
I wonder at the beauty and the talents all around me
I wonder at the love and dedication I see in so many
I wonder at the many amazing coincidences you create effortlessly

I can see how my effort is puny compared to your power
I can see how it serves me to put all my work in your hands

I can see how it serves me to put myself in your hands Dear God
I can see that your knowing and you wisdom is far greater than mine
I can feel your love for me in many wondrous ways
Things always work out for me, and I know that is because of you
Many wondrous things happen to bring me what I want
I like knowing that I am so well loved Dear God
I like knowing that I am the object of your constant attention
I like knowing that things are always working out for me because you are making them work
I wonder at how much you must love me Dear God to give me all that I have
Thank you God for everything. I love you. I love life.

Word of the day

Possibility

www.zmahoon.com

69. Possibility

Dear God thank you for this brand new day with brand new possibilities
I love knowing that anything is possible
I see evidence all around me that this is true
I see amazing things happening
I see people performing amazing physical feats, because they are open to possibilities
I see people creating the most amazing art forms and gadgets because they are open to possibilities
I see how powerful and versatile nature is and all things are possible
I have seen plants grow out of rocks
I have seen massive rocks balanced perfectly on an insignificant little tip
So many things that I use every day came to be because someone was open to their possibility
I love and appreciate many such things, electricity, the internet, my car, my computer, my microwave, my cell phone… at one time they were just possibilities and now they are manifest
Indeed everything starts with a possibility

There is a possibility that today will be a day full of synchronicities that lead me closer to all the things I want
There is a possibility that the abundance and success that is waiting for me will surprise me one day soon
There is a possibility that the loving relationship I want is going to rendezvous with me one day soon
There is a possibility that many wonderful things that I have forgotten about are going to surprise me every day
There is a possibility that I am doing better than I think I am
I see how being open to all possibilities is the path of least resistance

I see how things can turn around really quickly once I accept the possibility that they can
I see how it is as easy to create a castle as it is to create a button

Today I want to be open to all possibilities
I want to listen to my inner guidance and allow it to lead me to those possibilities that will give me the most joy
I know Dear God, that you know everything that I want and think about
I know that my work is to practice the art of allowing
I am ready Dear God, I am ready to accept that anything is possible and that all good things are lined up for me
I am ready to do the work, to offer the appreciation, to feel the joy that creates the crack through which all good things can come
Thank you Dear God for your love and your guidance. I love you. I love life. I love knowing that all things that I want are possible, not only possible but probable, not only probable but certain.
I am ready Dear God, I am ready for all possibilities

Word of the day

Impact

www.zmahoon.com

70. Impact

Dear God, thank you for this beautiful sunny day
I love waking up to a feeling of eagerness about what is to unfold
Today I have that feeling and it feels good
Today I know my ability to make an impact upon my future
Today I know my ability to make an impact upon people I love
Today I know my ability to make an impact on the world
And I am excited about this ability

I make an impact when I feel good
I make an impact when I focus with appreciation
I make an impact when I allow my natural zest for life
I make an impact when I allow my curiosity and creativity
I make an impact when I allow myself to feel free
I make an impact when I create castles in my mind
I make an impact when I look for the good in everything that happens
I make an impact when I look for the good in everyone around me
I make an impact when I appreciate nature
I make an impact when I hug my dog and pet my cat
I make an impact because of the thoughts I think
I make an impact by creating new things and ideas
I make an impact when I allow the Universal forces to bring my ideas to fruition
I make an impact when I allow myself to be who I am
I make an impact when I allow others to be who they are
I make an impact when I hold myself in an unconditional place

All that means is to be free flowing
It means feeling at peace at all times
It means knowing what to do when I don't

It means knowing that my work is to always look for a better feeling thought
It means being easy on myself and others
It means appreciating the little things in life
It means understanding the power of appreciation
It means understanding that every thought is a prayer
It means thinking and creating deliberately and consciously
It means paying attention to how I feel in every moment
Dear God, thank you for bringing me to this place of knowing
Thank you for helping me understand that I can make an impact
Thank you for the love you are always sending my way
I love You. I love life.

Word of the day

Enjoy!

www.zmahoon.com

71. Enjoy

Dear God, Thank you for this beautiful new day
Today I want to enjoy every moment of my day
I understand that looking for joy in every moment is a decision
I am making that decision
I want to be one who always looks for and finds joy
I want to be happy
I want to feel satisfaction
I know that I can find joy in everything
I know that I can enjoy a blue sky as much as I can enjoy a gray sky
I can find reasons to appreciate anything
There are so many things that are easy to appreciate
Like my puppy
It's so easy to appreciate her
She is so in love with life
Every morning she sees the world for the very first time
She teaches me to look at the world with wonder
Every snow flake is new and exciting through her eyes
Every leaf is a new toy through her eyes
She wants to romp and play and have fun
She is always excited to see me
She is always excited to see other people
Everyone she meets loves her because of her joyful energy
She is teaching me to enjoy looking at the beauty of the world through her eyes

Coffee is more satisfying in the morning when I focus on enjoying it
When I focus I notice its aroma, and flavor
When I focus I appreciate how warm it feels
When I focus I appreciate my mug

I acknowledge that my power of focus and my conscious use of it
Makes the difference between enjoyment and not
The more deliberate I am about where I apply my focus the more I enjoy things

Thank you Dear God for showing me how to enjoy the beauty of everything around me
I love you. I love life.

Word of the day

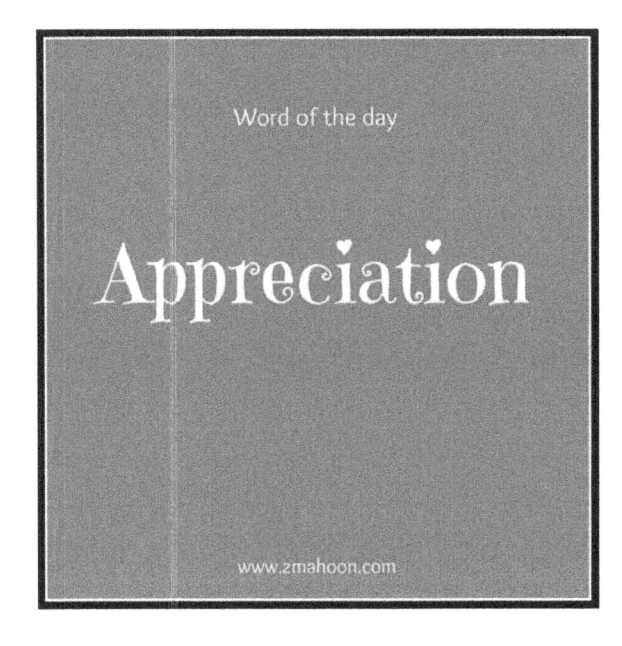

Appreciation

www.zmahoon.com

72. Appreciation

Dear God, Thank you for this brand new day
I love and appreciate this opportunity to have fun
I love and appreciate waking up and feeling fresh and full of energy
I love and appreciate my peaceful morning time when I can enjoy having the house to myself
I so appreciate the peace and quiet of an early morning
I so appreciate watching the sky change color as I sip my coffee and look out on to the trees
I so appreciate my morning meditation and pre-paving
I so appreciate my morning walk – feeling the crisp cold air on my face, feeling alive

I appreciate my beautiful children and the love that fills our lives
I appreciate my friends and co-creators and the interactions that make life interesting and fun
I appreciate me for all the work I've done and continue to do to improve my life, have clarity about how things work and help others do the same
I appreciate where I am today; I am in a really good place, I have improved so many things in my life
I appreciate the peace I feel within and most of all I appreciate knowing how to think and feel

Today I want to appreciate a few special people in my life, who have helped me to truly understand unconditional love, how to practice it, how to feel it, and how to teach it – thank you for helping me grow. I love you.
Today I want to look for and find more opportunities to appreciate
I want to be conscious of all the good things in my life, all the beautiful people who will co-create with me, all the magnificent things I will see, the delicious food I will taste, and the satisfying work I will do

I know that appreciation is the key to everything that I want and I know that when I appreciate I just feel so good and really that is all that I want
I want to feel good
I want to be guided to following my guidance towards thoughts of appreciation, thoughts that feel good
Thank you for my heart that is so full of love
Thank you for the peace I feel within
Thank you for the gift of life. I love you. I love life.

Word of the day

Inspiration

www.zmahoon.com

73. Inspiration

Dear God, Thank you for this brand new day
Today I want to feel inspired in everything I do
I love the feeling of inspiration
I love feeling the energy moving through my body when I experience inspired thought
I love the clarity of an inspired thought
I love how sure it feels

When I feel inspired I know that it is time to take action – time to follow my inspiration
I like knowing that I know how to find my alignment and reach that place where inspiration can come
I feel lit up when I am in that space
Things comes easy when I am in that space
Words flow easily when I am in that space
I like knowing that I can focus with intensity, and when I apply that sort of focus inspiration is sure to come
I like knowing that all I have to do is to start this sort of rampage of appreciation and pretty soon I find myself in that space
I like knowing that I wake up in that space
I like knowing that I sleep in that space
I like knowing that there is an unlimited supply of inspired thought that I can tap into
I like knowing that as I offer words of appreciation I am priming the pump that will allow inspiration to flow
Life feels so good knowing that I have control
I love the power of knowing that I am a deliberate creator and I can pick my words in a manner that serves me

I like knowing that I can change the way I feel and that my manifestations tell me how I'm doing
I like knowing that there is always more to want and more of life to enjoy
I like knowing that life is easy and life is meant to be fun
I like knowing that I can feel my connection with You Dear God

I can feel that connection viscerally
I can feel it in the movement of my body
I can feel it in the clarity of my thought
I know I am inspired when the perfect idea flows into my mind and is translated to words with ease and I know that it was perfect in every way – perfect words, perfect delivery, perfect reception
I love that feeling and I want more of it
I want to spend my day in the space where inspired thought is my habit of thought
I love the feeling of inspiration and I want to be one who is a source of inspiration for others
I want to be an up-lifter and a teacher
I want to be the conduit through which inspiration flows freely
Thank you for this day Dear God. Today I will focus on allowing a feeling of inspiration
I will celebrate being inspired. I will celebrate my connection with You. I love you. I love life.

Word of the day

Fantastic!

www.zmahoon.com

74. Fantastic!

Dear God, Thank you for the opportunity to create a fantastic day
I know that appreciation is the key to creation, when I appreciate each moment of my day is fantastic
I really do have a fantastic life

I have been to many places and met many fantastic people
I have seen many beautiful things, and had many fantastic accomplishments
I have first hand evidence in my life that fantastic things can happen
I remember the time when I drove all over Ontario with the gas cap sitting on the back of my car – that was fantastic
I remember the time when I created the Warapples franchise out of nothing – that was fantastic
I remember the manner in which I found my job at the bank – that was fantastic
I remember playing the shopping cart game and getting a free cart every time – that was fantastic
I can remember so many fantastic things that have happened for me in the past

It's wonderful to know that I created them all with my thought
It's wonderful to know that I am getting better and better at creating and allowing
It's wonderful to know that all things are possible
It's wonderful to know that many fantastic things are waiting to happen for me
I like the evidence of my alignment

I like knowing that I can change my thoughts in any moment
I like knowing that I know how to think pure positive thoughts

I like thinking about and visualizing many aspects of my future
I like knowing that I can visualize many fantastic things just for the fun of it
I like knowing that I don't have to make things happen
I like knowing that my job is simply to have fun and as long as I am having fun fantastic things are on their way
I like knowing that I can find something fantastic to appreciate about every person I meet and co-create with
I like knowing that I can find something fantastic to appreciate about everything I do, at home and at work

I want more fantastic things to appreciate everyday
I want fantastic to be the norm in my life
I want a fantastic day everyday Dear God
Please guide me to make all my days fantastic and full of love and joy
I love you. I love life.

Word of the day

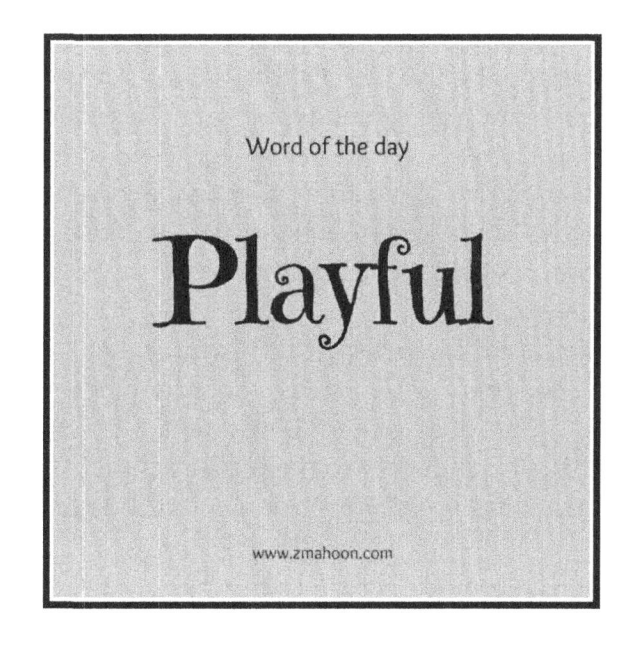

Playful

www.zmahoon.com

75. Playful

Dear God, Thank you for this beautiful brand new day
I feel happy and excited today, ready to enjoy my day
I feel playful and light hearted and full of life
I feel good, life is good and there is so much to love and appreciate
I love and appreciate each and every person who attends meditation with me on Tuesday nights
I love the playful attitude of everyone at our meet-up
I love the laughter and the friendships that have come about because of it
I love and appreciate my children and their capacity to play and have fun all the time
I love their ability to derive pleasure from simple everyday things
And I absolutely love and adore how they play together
It warms my heart to feel the love and the laughter with which they co-create
I love the playfulness with which my cats live each day
It is wonderful to see them get excited over little things
Truly, extracting joy out of a moment is just a matter of perspective
I am blessed to be surrounded by so many examples of playfulness
reminding me that I have the ability to don an attitude of play at anytime

I choose to be playful today
I choose to see the world as a happy place with many opportunities to have fun and play
I choose to be light hearted and open
I choose to love
I choose to trust
I choose to be happy
I choose to be open to Your guidance Dear God

Today I want to teach from the clarity of my own experience the idea of playfulness
I want to show everyone around me that an attitude of play makes the journey easy and fun
I want to show everyone that playfulness and joy are a choice
I want to remember to make that choice in every moment of everyday
Thank you God for the joy in my life. I love you. I love life.

Word of the day

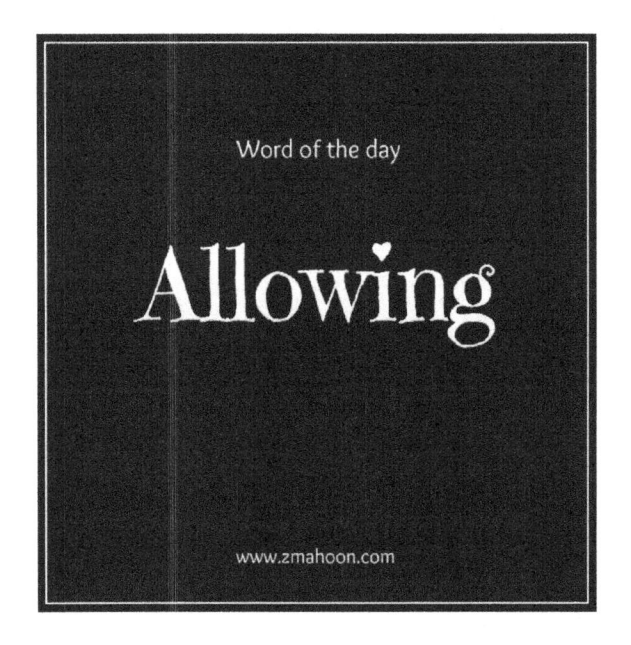

Allowing

www.zmahoon.com

76. Allowing

Dear God, Thank you for this brand new day
My word for today is "allowing"
I love the feeling of allowing my wellbeing
I can feel the joy of allowing; it feels like energy flowing
I like the feeling of flowing energy
I can see the evidence around me that tells me that allowing is the natural way of things
I can see that all animals and plants allow their wellbeing
I can see that there is a continuous cycle of life in nature that is based on allowing
I can see that all things in nature allow You Dear God to have your way with them
And I can see that your plan for everything is always the best plan of all
I can see that all things in nature allow your plan to unfold effortlessly

The sun always rises easily, water always flows easily
Seasons change, new replaces old all the time
Acceptance and allowing are the mantra of everything in nature
And I can see how acceptance of your greater wisdom and allowing of your design is the only path to joy
Here I am Dear God, ready to allow my wellbeing
Today I want to be like the water that flows in the rivers and the streams and the little brooks

I love how water always finds a way to flow towards its Source
I love the ease with which water flows, whenever something gets in its way, water always finds a way around it or under it or over it – water allows itself to be guided. I want to be like that.

Water is always finding the path of ease, the path of least resistance, the path of allowing
Water has power too; water can be strong, and beautiful, and cheerful and sparkly
I love water. I love the sound of water as it flows
I love gazing at running water in the streams and I love watching the waves come in at the beaches
I love being on water, and I love being in water – I absolutely love and adore water
Today I want to focus on the subject of allowing and feel like a little brook flowing towards its Source
I want to look for the path of allowing in all things that I do today
I want to allow the flow of abundance and health and joy
I want to feel the feeling of ease that comes with allowing
I want to feel the feeling of allowing my guidance to lead me to all good things
I want to feel the feeling of allowing wellbeing
Thank you God for all my blessings. I love you. I love life.

Word of the day

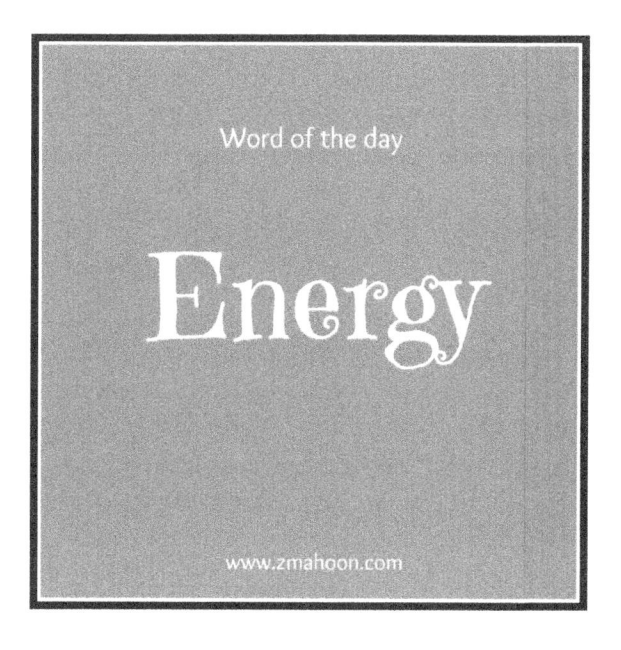

Energy

www.zmahoon.com

77. Energy

Dear God, Thank you for another brand new day
I love waking up feeling energized and happy
I love stretching and feeling my body waking up
I love consciously flowing energy from the top of my head right down to the tips of my toes
Flowing energy makes me feel alive – it's good to feel alive

I like knowing that my energy connects me with everything in this world and with the non-physical
I like knowing that the energy flowing through me is the energy that creates worlds
I like knowing that I control the flow of energy
I like knowing that my thoughts are a form of energy and I can turn thoughts to things
I like playing with my energy to have fun with creating
It is fun to create things just for the pleasure of creating
I like knowing that I am a powerful creator and my energy is my medium
Thank you God for showing me that appreciation makes energy flow
I like the ease and flow of energy and I enjoy living in a constant state of appreciation
I like the energy and the stamina of my physical body

I enjoy the energy of my thinking process
I love the sudden rush of energy when a new idea occurs to me
I love the energy I feel inside me when I help someone to a new place of clarity
I love that I know what to do to ramp up my energy
I love knowing that there is no end to the energy that flows – it is always there and I can plug into it consciously

That's what I want dear God, I want to be one who is connected to my Source of energy

I want to be one who is conscious of that connection
I want to be one who knows what to do to ramp it up
Today I want to flow the energy of love to everyone and all things around me
Today I want to feel the clarity of thought that comes with flowing energy
Today I want to feel energized and alert
Flowing energy makes me feel one with the world and I love that feeling of oneness
Today I want to allow the flow of energy to improve all subjects in my life
Thank you for this beautiful day Dear God. I love you. I love life. I love my energy.

Word of the day

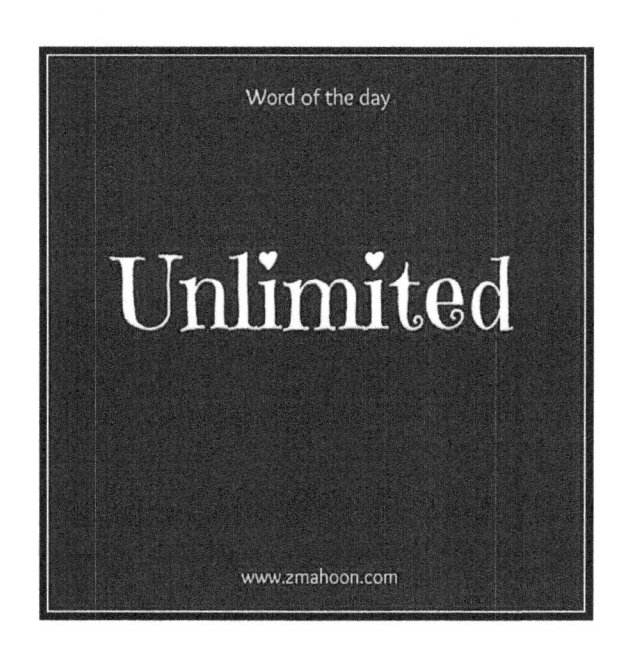

Unlimited

www.zmahoon.com

78. Unlimited

Dear God, thank you for this wonderful new day
A day with unlimited possibilities
Today I am open to whatever comes
Today I am feeling the ease and flow of life
I understanding that there is unlimited wellbeing in the world
Unlimited wellbeing for me and for everyone else
We can each have everything we want
God grants all wishes
There is an unlimited supply of everything if we believe it
I am unlimited – I can have, be or do anything I want

Unlimited joy
Unlimited laughter
Unlimited love
Unlimited resources
Unlimited wealth
Unlimited health
Unlimited stamina
Unlimited capacity to learn and grow
Unlimited peace
Unlimited creativity
Unlimited, unlimited, unlimited…

I am unlimited
I can have, be or do anything I want
My life has the unlimited capacity to yield anything I think about
I like the feeling of being unlimited
It feels like freedom
It feels open

It feels abundant
It feels like energy flowing
All of nature is teaching me that God's love is unlimited
God never holds back love from any creation
Thank you Dear God for your unlimited love
Thank you for the unlimited guidance you keep sending my way
Thank you for the unlimited blessings in my life
Thank you for the unlimited joy in my life
I love You. I love life.

Word of the day

Embrace

www.zmahoon.com

79. Embrace

Good Morning world
Today is going to be a good day
Today I am open to receiving all good things that God has lined up for me
I know that God always wants what's good
I know that it is up to me to allow good things into my life
I am ready to open my heart and embrace all that is good in this world
I embrace all people as my equal; we are all the same
Everyone wants joy and freedom and love, just like I do
I embrace all animals and birds
We come from the same Source
I love and appreciate the variety that they add
I appreciate how accepting they are of everything
I appreciate the beautifully coloured feathers on birds
But most of all I appreciate how birds trust that they will always find food and they do

I want to be like the birds and trust that I will always find what I am looking for
I want to embrace my guidance and allow it to lead me to that which is good for me
I appreciate everything that God has provided for me
I have wonderful friends and family
I have work that provides for me and my family
I have good health and vitality

I have beautiful children
I love where I live
I love my freedom and my ability to go where I want to go and do what I want to do

I love my life and I am ready to embrace new things
I am ready to embrace new ideas
I am open to learning and growing
I am happy to embrace change for it keeps life interesting
Change keeps me focused on the future, I like that
Thank you Dear God for everything I have
I am willing and happy to embrace all things and people and events that come to me
For I have learnt that there is good in all things
Today I embrace change and welcome everything that comes with it
I love life. I love me.

Word of the day

Shine

www.zmahoon.com

80. Shine

Rise and shine are perfect words
Today is my day to shine
Thank you Dear God for this opportunity to enjoy life

I want to be present in every moment today
I want to find something to appreciate in every moment
I want to focus my thoughts consciously
I want You to shine your light upon me and guide me through all my decisions, big and small
I want to be guided as much in ordering a pizza as choosing job
I want my path to light up with every step I take
I want to find peace in my heart knowing that all paths lead to where I want to go

I want to find joy in the company of the people I love
I want to find satisfaction in the work I do
I want to find something to appreciate everywhere I turn
I want to demonstrate the power of positive thought
I want to shine with the eagerness of living life
Today is my day to shine
I want to shine brighter than the sun and the stars
I want to shine in everything I do
I want my inner sunshine to light up my heart
I want my inner sunshine to light up my smile
I want to embrace everything that happens in my world with the knowing that all is well
I know all is well
I know that Your love and light are always shining down upon me
I know that You are always leading me towards my greater wellbeing

There is good in everything and everyone
Today I want to shine with zest for life
Today I want to have fun
I want to love life and enjoy my day
Thank you Dear God for this opportunity to shine
I love you. I love life, and today is my day to shine.

Word of the day

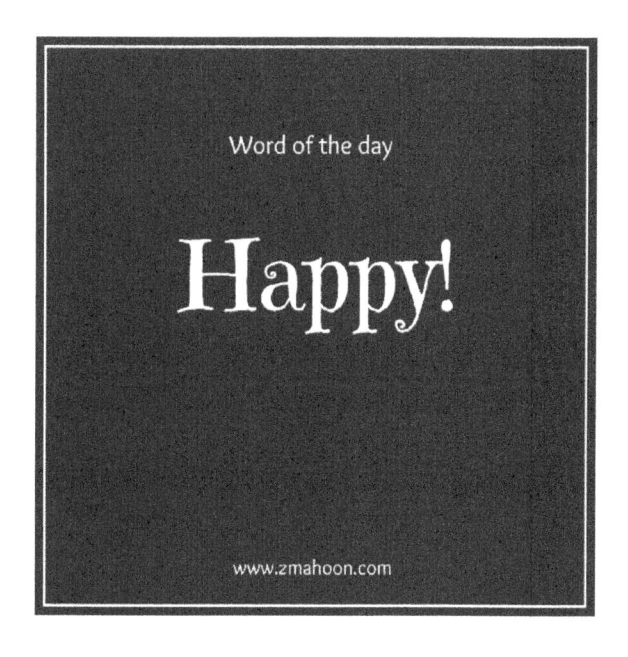

Happy!

www.zmahoon.com

81. Happy!

Dear God, Thank you for this brand new day
Thank you for all the wonderful things in my life that make me happy
It makes me happy to gaze at my son's peaceful face as he sleeps beside me
I like it when he snuggles into my bed in the morning and hugs me tight
It makes me happy when I look out and see the tall trees in my backyard reaching for the sky
It makes me happy to watch the sunrise, washing the sky in many amazing colors
It makes me happy to appreciate nature, I love trees and water, and sky. I love rocks and Earth and flowers.
It makes me happy when my cats gives me a tongue bath
It makes me happy when I see happy smiles on people, especially children
It makes me happy to feel all my blessings

I am happy with who I am and who I am becoming
I am happy with where I am and where I am going
I am happy with all my accomplishments and my talents
I am happy with the health and prosperity that is flowing into my life with ease
I am happy with the journey that has brought me to where I am
I am happy that I have grown in many ways, and I love all the co-creators who have contributed to my journey – I love them all
I am happy with the peace I feel in my heart today
I am happy trusting you Dear God, happy knowing that you are always with me, supporting me, guiding me, loving me, helping me

I want to be a deliberate creator, thinking thoughts that lead me towards happiness and joy on all subjects in my life

I want to co-create happy loving relationships with my children, my friends and my partner
I want to be happy with the work I do, knowing that I add value
I want to be happy today and I want to look for things that make me happier still
I want to end this day feeling happy and satisfied in every way
Thank you Dear God for the love and happiness and peace in my life. I love you. I love life.

Word of the day

Contentment

www.zmahoon.com

82. Contentment

Dear God, thank you for this brand new day.
Today my word of the day is contentment.
Please bless my heart with contentment.
Contentment with everything around me and within me
Contentment in knowing that I have your love and your guidance at all times
Contentment in knowing that I have figured out the meaning of unconditional love

Thank you for showing me how to love unconditionally
Thank you for loving me unconditionally
Thank you for the peace I feel within me
Thank you for the contentment in knowing that all is truly well
Thank you for the contentment in knowing that I can leave all my cares to you while I apply myself to enjoying the moment I am in now.
Thank you for my beautiful children, I feel content when I think about them
Thank you for the love in my heart that is overflowing because of them, and benefiting me and all those around me
Thank you for giving me this invaluable gift of a loving heart

Today I want to co-create with others in joy and contentment
Thank you for the strength I feel inside me because I am so sure of your love and your guidance
Thank you for always helping me find a better feeling thought
Thank you for always guiding me on my path.
I want to start this day with contentment filling my heart
I want to end this day feeling completely satisfied with myself and my achievements - content in every way
I want to feel the contentment that comes from loving and from being loved

I want to feel the contentment of prosperity
I want to feel the contentment of good health
I want to feel the contentment of feeling worthy at all times
I want to feel the contentment of knowing that there is always perfect timing in all things
I turn my day over to you from this point on Dear God.
Trusting that all is always well, trusting your love and your guidance
Trusting that you will guide me toward all those things that are good for me
Trusting that I will know when it is time for me to act and when it is time for me to rest
I want to feel the contentment of being where I am
I want to feel the eagerness of knowing that many good things are lined up for me.
Thank you Dear God - thank you for everything. I love you. I love life.

Word of the day

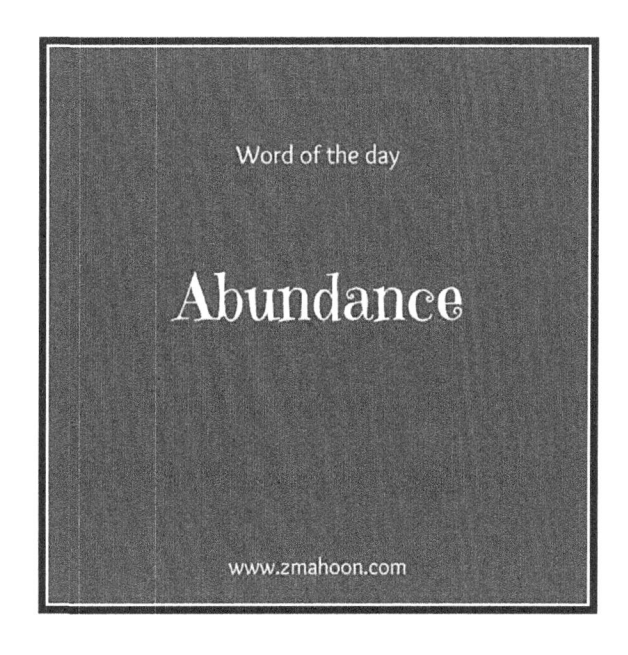

Abundance

www.zmahoon.com

83. Abundance

Dear God, Thank you for this brand new day.
Thank you for the abundance of wellbeing in the Universe.
Thank you for the abundance of air and water and space.
Thank you for signs in nature that are showing me that abundance is the natural order of things
I love feeling a feeling of abundance

Abundance feels like ease and flow, in and out, never ending, ever flowing energy
Abundance feels like the ease and flow of breathing air in and breathing it out
Abundance feels like water in the oceans, always more, always flowing, never ending
Abundance feels like the joy of a good meal shared with friends, with lots of left overs
Abundance feels like lots of laughter, there is always more where that came from
Abundance feels like good friends always ready to put their arms around you
Abundance feels like the love I feel for my children, ever flowing, ever giving
Abundance feels like the joy of buying new things and bringing them home
Abundance feels like giving generously and feeling happy about it
Abundance feels like a relaxed day at home in my hammock watching the clouds float by
Abundance feels like ever flowing words and more things to talk about and write about
Abundance feels like joy I feel when I see beautiful things
Abundance feels like the joy I feel when I see people in love

Abundance feels like the wonder I feel when I see tall mountains and open fields
Abundance feels like a field full of wheat, shining golden in the sunlight
Abundance feels like sunlight, there is always more

I love the abundance of the world I live in
I love the abundance of many things in my life, and I want more of that
I want to feel my financial prosperity and abundance
I want to feel my never ending capacity for love
I want to feel the energy of my Source flowing through my body
I want to feel my wellbeing and the wellbeing of the world
Today I want to notice and appreciate all the signs of abundance around me
I want to appreciate abundance in nature
I want to appreciate people who have created a life of ease and abundance for themselves
I want more abundance
I want an abundance of joy, an abundance of love, an abundance of health and an abundance of money in my life
Dear God, please guide me towards my greater wellbeing, and show me the path of ease towards an abundance of all good things in my life. I love you. I love life.

Word of the day

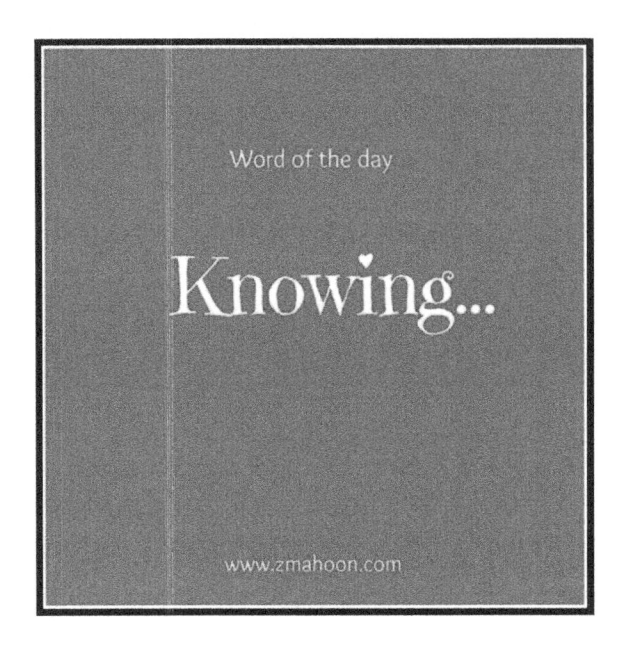

Knowing...

www.zmahoon.com

84. Knowing

Dear God, Thank you for this brand new day.
I love waking up feeling happy and relaxed.
I love knowing that I am always loved
I love knowing that things are always working out for me
I love knowing that I am a powerful creator and I can have, be or do anything I want
I love knowing that I only have to focus on this one day and make the best of it
I love knowing that all is well in my world
I love knowing that I always have guidance
I love knowing that there is perfect timing for everything
I love knowing that universal forces are working for me making my path easy
I love knowing that my work is to have fun
I love knowing that all I have to do is to be a lover, and I am that
I love life, I flow my love to everyone and everything around me
I love loving
I love knowing that there are countless things that are working really well in my life
I love knowing that there are unlimited possibilities
I love knowing that I have come a long way in my knowing…
Today I want to feel the ease and flow of abundance
Today I want to feel the ease and flow of love
Today I want to know my wellbeing
Today please help me know where I must go, what I must do, and what I must say so that I can be one who creates deliberately
Today please help me be closer to the manifestation of my desires
Today please help me feel peace within
Thank you God. I love you. I love life.

Word of the day

Incredible

www.zmahoon.com

85. Incredible

Dear God, thank you for this brand new day.
It is delicious to wake up in the warm cocoon of my covers
I love stretching and feeling my body come alive
I love feeling the comfort of my bed
I love feeling relaxed and happy
I love contemplating the incredible things that nature is showing me today like the incredible sunrise
The sounds of the world waking up

It is incredible that the sun always rises without any effort, and that the Earth silently completes its spinning and circling, and that I can always trust these things as signs that You are always looking after everything
It is incredible that the systems of this world run so smoothly everyday for billions of years past and more to come
It is incredible that a huge tree was once a tiny seed
And that my big boy was once a tiny baby

It is incredible that my body functions without my conscious involvement
It is incredible that people are so creative, all the way from the making of the first wheel to the making of the complex gadgets we use every day
It is incredible that when I think of someone, they call me or write to me
It is incredible that You always find a way for me to progress
It is incredible that there are always more solutions and options than I can think of at any time

Life is an incredible gift
It is incredible that I have learnt so much and changed my life in so many ways

I am incredible! I realize that I am an incredible being. I have power and my desires are important
My joy is important

Dear God, please help me see the evidence of your incredible love for me and for this world and it's people as I go about my day today.
I want to see myself as an incredible being who has value.
I want to see others as incredible beings as well, who have value and are seeking love, joy and freedom in the same way that I am seeking these things

I know that you are powerful because you show me your incredible power every day, and I know that all I have to do is to put my faith in you and follow your guidance for it will surely lead me to the love, joy and freedom that I seek.
Please help me along my way. Help me to feel the incredible well-being that You have bestowed upon me. I want to feel your love for me and for this planet and all mankind.
I know I am incredibly worthy and many incredible things are waiting to unfold before me – and for me
I can feel that I am well on my way.
Thank you God for your incredible love. I love you. I love life.

Word of the day

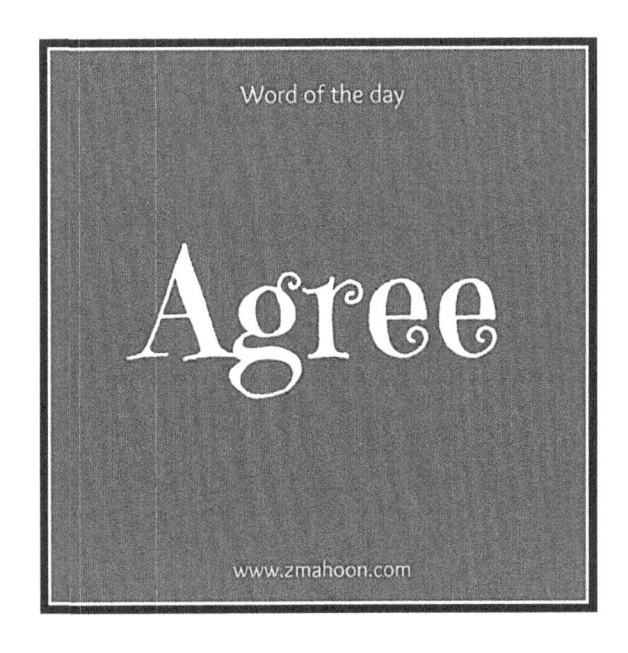

Agree

www.zmahoon.com

86. Agree

Dear God, thank you for another amazing day
I agree that I am responsible for what happens to me today and everyday
I agree that my thoughts create my reality
I agree that I can control my thoughts and therefore I can control what I create
I agree that the emotion accompanying my thought tells me what I am creating
I agree that when I think good feeling thoughts I am creating good things
I agree that thoughts of appreciation feel good
I agree that when I appreciate I feel happier
I agree that I can always find something to appreciate and feel good about
Today I feel good about simple little everyday things

I feel good thinking about the perfect parking spot that I manifest at work everyday
I feel good thinking about my dog greeting me with excitement when I come home
I feel good thinking about my children and their beautiful smiling faces
I feel good thinking about cats purring next to me
I feel good thinking about the massage I have lined up next week
I feel good thinking about the holiday that is just around the corner
I feel good thinking about the good food we eat everyday
I feel good when I look around me and appreciate my surroundings, my warm and cozy living room

The big maple tree outside my window
The squirrels that scamper up and down its big trunk
The glimpses of blue sky through its dense leaves and branches
The sunshine streaming in through the windows

It feels like the perfect day for a perfect day
Today I want to set the tone for each interaction with others by appreciating something about them
Today I want to appreciate my employers before I start work
Today I want to appreciate my abundance before I eat and appreciate my body for knowing what to do with everything I give it
Today I want to feel love for my children before I talk to them or hug them
Today I want to appreciate my car for giving me such good service
Today I want to appreciate my friends for always being there for me
Today I want to appreciate the work I do for it allow me the opportunity to feel good
Today I want to appreciate Abraham for their teachings, as well as all my other teachers
Today I want to appreciate the sound of music and the sound of birds
I am understanding now that only good things come to me when I am in a state of appreciation
Thank you God for helping me to understand how the universe works and how prayers are answered
Thank you for your everlasting guidance and love. I love you. I love life.

Word of the day

Fun!

www.zmahoon.com

87. Fun!

Dear God, thank you for this brand new day.
I love waking up feeling refreshed
I love the aroma of my morning coffee
I love holding my favourite mug and feeling it warm my hands
I absolutely love my first sip of coffee in the morning
It makes me feel so alive, ready for my new day

I love the warmth inside me as I drink my coffee and look at the trees in my backyard
I love the trees in my back yard, I love trees
I love how beautiful they are and I love their silent participation in the world
I love how trees stand rooted in their faith and allow everything they need to come to them
I love watching the sun rise fill the sky with a burst of color
It fills my heart with joy
It makes me feel the power of universal forces that orchestrate the working of the world
I love thinking that my job in this world is just to have fun

Today I want to look for fun in everything I do
Today I want to don the perspective of fun
Today I want to take fun with me wherever I go
I want all who co-create with me to feel the energy of fun
I want to spread the feeling of joy and fun all around
I want to feel the fun of basking in my own sunshine
I want to feel my alignment
I want to feel the all is wellness of the world
I want to remember to seek and find joy as I go about my day
I want to smile and laugh and love

I want to contribute towards making the world a happy place
Dear God, I want your help in remembering that I can always choose an attitude of joy and fun
And that when I am having fun, I am on my way towards all the things I want.
Thank you God for this brand new day. I love you. I love life.

Word of the day

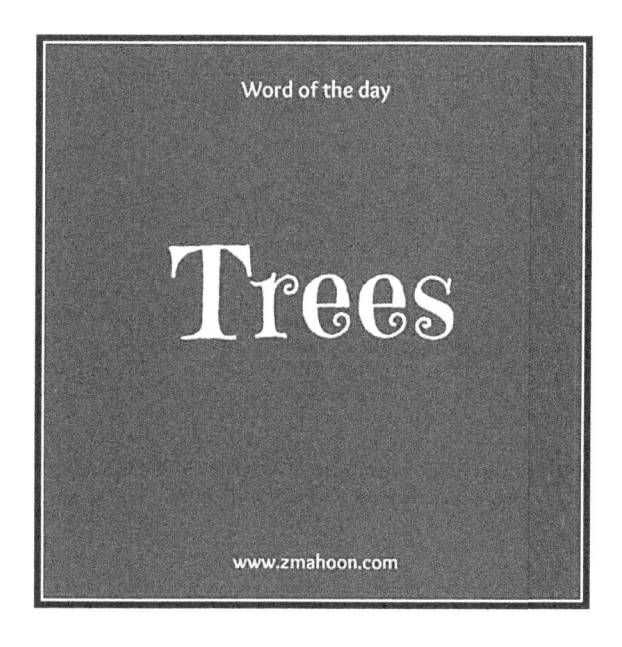

Trees

www.zmahoon.com

88. Trees

Dear God, thank you for a wonderful new day
I love waking up and gazing at the trees from my bed
I love trees
Trees are my best friends
I have learnt so much from my friends
Today I want to offer appreciation for my silent friends
I always look at trees as an example of faith
Trees never pick up their roots and go running looking for the things they want
They always stand rooted in their faith that everything they need will come to them
And it does

I always look at trees as an example of abundance
Trees are always giving of them selves
They give us fruits
They give us shade
They give us beauty
They give us wood
They give animals a place to rest and hide
They hold the earth in its place
They believe that they will never be less because of their giving
And they never are
I always look at trees as an example of complete allowing
Trees always let God and nature and man have their way
Trees never push back against anything
Trees never hold a grudge
They never fuss
Trees submit to the changing weather

Trees submit to whatever comes their way
As a result they always grow
Trees understand their place in the cycle of life

They come to life, always reaching for the sun
Growing, growing, growing and then making way for new ones
They understand that there is never any need to hand on to anything or anyone
They do their work silently, helping to keep our environment clean
They never ask for credit
They live in harmony with all other trees and beings
They always look perfect no matter what they are wearing
They never compare
They just are
Thank you dear trees for showing us what it means to have faith
I love you. I love life.

Word of the day

Praise

www.zmahoon.com

89. Praise

Dear God, thank you for another wonderful beginning
Each day is a new opportunity to start all over again
So much can happen in just one day, so much can change in just one day
Truly anything is possible
I am beginning to understand that my role is to praise and appreciate

Praise the Lord, I was taught, but I never really understood why and how
It seemed silly that the All Mighty God would need my praise
But now I understand that I am the one who needs the praise
I understand now that when I praise my life improves
I am learning to look at my life differently
I am learning that when I offer praise for all the wonderful things in my life
Life keeps getting better and better and better
I understand now that when I feel the open feeling of appreciation and praise
It generates a powerful positive energy that makes all good things possible for me
And so I offer praise

I offer praise not because you need me to Dear God
I offer praise because I need what it does for me
I offer praise because it enables me to receive your love
I offer praise for my own diligence in figuring this out
I offer praise for all the good things in my life
I offer praise for the help and guidance that I know is always there for me
I offer praise for the beauty of the universe
I offer praise for the intricacy of life
I offer praise for the Earth and the Sun and the Moon
I offer praise for the food I eat

I offer praise for progress and diversity
I offer praise for what is gone and what is becoming
I offer praise for the powerful working of the universe
The clouds, the rain, the snow, and the changing seasons
I offer praise for the beautiful colors and shapes of flowers
I offer praise for me eyes that can see far and wide
I offer praise for the miracle of life that I enjoy everyday
Thank you Dear God for all the wonderful things in my life
I love You. I love life.

Word of the day

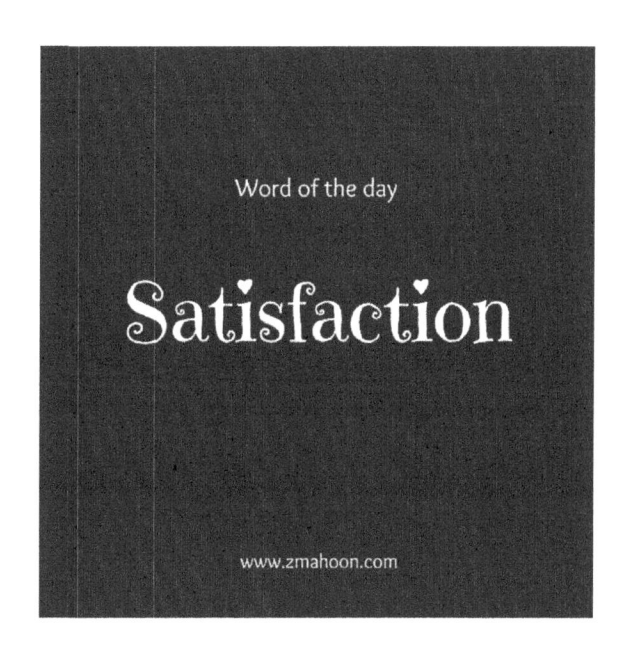

Satisfaction

www.zmahoon.com

90. Satisfaction

Dear God, thank you for this beautiful brand new day.
Thank you for all the wonderful things in my life.
I find so much satisfaction in loving my children and enjoying their laughter and watching them thrive
I find so much satisfaction in cooking a good meal and watching it being enjoyed

Thank you for the satisfaction I feel after a day well spent at work
Thank you for the satisfaction I feel when money flows into my experience with ease and flow
I love the feeling of satisfaction in meeting all my commitments financial and otherwise

I love the feeling of satisfaction I feel in helping others
I love the feeling of satisfaction I feel as a teacher
I love the feeling of satisfaction in always doing my best
I love the feeling of satisfaction in creating new things
I love the feeling of satisfaction I feel in writing and teaching
I love the satisfaction of a good nights' sleep
I love the satisfaction of knowing that all is well
I love the satisfaction of knowing that You are always guiding me, helping me

Today I want to look for satisfaction everywhere I go, in everything I do and all the interactions I have
Today I want to feel the satisfaction of knowing that I'm really figuring out how law of attraction works and I am beginning to apply it consciously for my greater good

Today I want to feel the satisfaction that comes when the universe shows me the evidence of my alignment
Today I want to feel good. Thank you for this day Dear God. I love you. I love life.

Word of the day

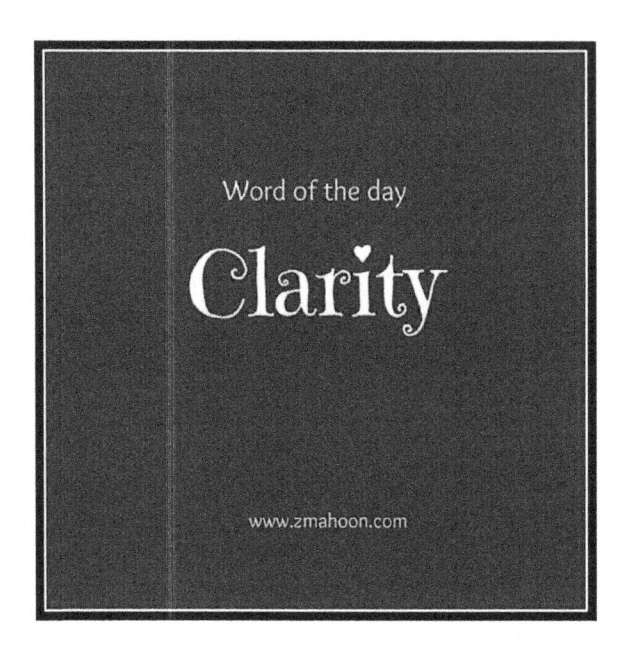

Clarity

www.zmahoon.com

91. Clarity

Dear God, thank you for this brand new day.
Thank you for the vitality and the clarity that I feel today.
Thank you for the clear blue skies and the sun that shines
Reminding me that there are so many things that you look after for me on a daily basis
It is a nice reminder to think that the things I desire are easy compared to the rising of the sun and the movement of the planets – I like knowing that
I like being clear minded. I like being decisive.
I like the feeling of energy flowing when I am clear minded – it feels like being alive

It feels like the clarity of water as it flows in the streams and the rivers
It feels like the clarity of blue skies and sunshine
It feels like the clean clear movement of cutting veges when I cook
It feels like the satisfaction of sparkling clear clean floors
It feels like the joy of a decision well made

I want to feel this sort of clarity in everything I do today
I want to feel clear minded and alert
I want to feel the power of my ability to focus and draw to me the answers and solutions that I need
I want to feel the clarity of the next step along my path
I want to feel the clarity of the guidance that I know is always there
I want to feel the clarity and depth of the love you feel for me
I want to feel love for everyone and everything around me
Today I want to offer clear words to express my thoughts
I want to be clear minded and guided in everything I do
Today I will deliberately remind myself to ask for clarity of thought throughout my day

I will focus on feeling good because I know that when I feel good, clarity is easy
Thank you God for this beautiful day. I love you. I love life.

The word of the day

Trust

www.zmahoon.com

92. Trust

Dear God, thank you for this brand new day
I like the feeling of trust, knowing that there is always a new day
A brand new start, an opportunity to look at things differently
Thank you for my numerous blessings
Thank you for my knowing
Thank you for always guiding me towards my greater well being
I like trusting that things are always working out for me
I like trusting that all things in nature have guidance, and I too have guidance
I like trusting that my body knows what to do
I like trusting that I can train my mind to trust and receive guidance
Thank you for the guidance that is always coming to me

I trust that the sun will rise tomorrow
I trust that the stars will shine
I trust that the seasons will change
I trust that things never stay the same and that there is good in that
I trust that you know best
I trust that things always work out for me
I trust that there is abundance of all things
I trust that I will always find my way
I trust that people are good
I trust that the universe is unlimited
I trust the feeling inside me that tells me all is well
I like the feeling of trust

When I trust I feel satisfied
When I trust I am at peace
When I trust it is easy to be happy

When I trust it is easy be carefree
I love the joy that has come into my life
I want more of that
I want to feel good about all aspects of my life
I want to feel joy and freedom and love
I love you. I love life.

Word of the day

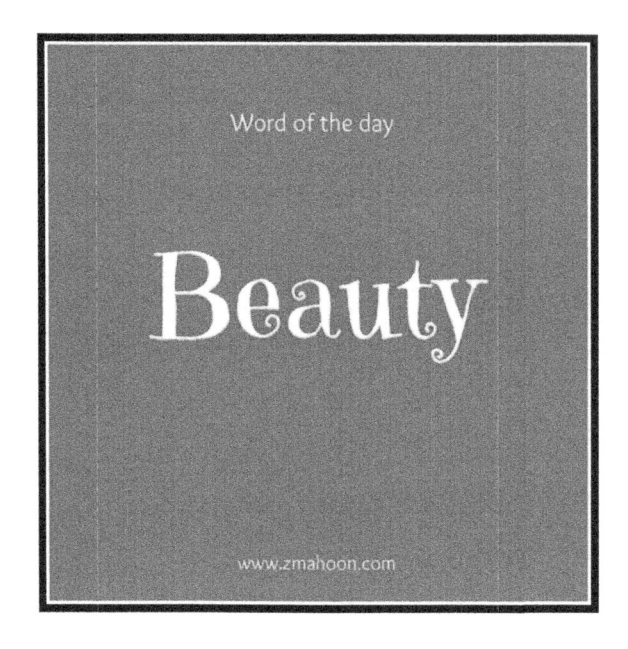

Beauty

www.zmahoon.com

93. Beauty

Dear God, Thank you for this beautiful new day
I love waking up to a day at home
It's nice to snuggle up and enjoy the warmth and relaxation of my bed
I love looking out on to the world when I wake up
It is a blessing to feast my eyes on the beautiful sky and the trees
The world is such a beautiful place

I love where I live. There is so much beauty here. I love the woods and forests and the water.
I love the contrast that the changing weather creates
I love the beauty of the white snow covered trees in the winter
And the beautiful greens in the summer, and I absolutely adore and drool over fall colors
I love the beauty of sunshine falling over water
I love the beauty of the different colors and shades all around me
I love the beauty in nature and in art and music
I love the creativity of people and the beautiful things they make

I see perfection in everything and beauty in everyone I meet
Everything in the world is an extension of you Dear God and therefore an extension of me
It feels good to think and feel that way
It feels good to know my own beauty, for I am an extension of God, everything about me is perfect
It feels good to know the beauty and perfection of my children and those I love
It feels good to know the beauty and perfection of those co-creators who instigate me towards growth and greater understanding
It feels good to find beauty in everything, and I like feeling good

I love my beautiful loving heart, I love loving
I feel the happiest when I am loving and receiving love
I want more of that, I want more love in my life, I want more joy, more beauty
I like sharing and co-creating; beauty is multiplied when appreciation is shared
I want that – I want to share my appreciation of the beauty of this world and its people with the people I love – together we are more, together our joy is multiplied

Thank you Dear God for showing me the beauty of co-creation
I want eyes that see only beauty in everyone and everything
I want ears that hear the beauty of all the sounds around me
I want hands that feel the beauty of all textures and shapes
I want to taste the deliciousness food that is beautiful in its presentation
I want to enjoy the beauty of delicious pleasing aromas
I want to be a perceiver of beauty
Perception of beauty leads to joy, and a feeling of appreciation
I love feeling joy and appreciation
Thank you Dear God for showing me how to appreciate the beauty of everything around me.
I love you. I love life.

The word of the day

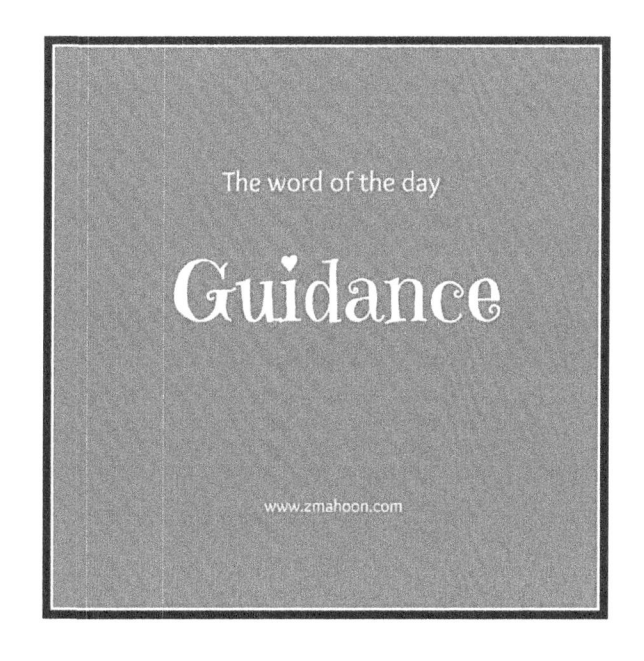

Guidance

www.zmahoon.com

94. Guidance

Thank you for the guidance that is always leading me towards my wellbeing
I love and appreciate my guidance that is always telling me that all is well
I love feeling the emotion that tells me when I'm lined up with Source and when I'm not
I love knowing that where I am today is perfect in every way
I love knowing that where ever I go and whatever I do, I have access to guidance from Source
I love knowing that all is truly well
I love knowing that all things in nature follow the guidance that comes from Source
I love knowing that when I follow guidance that feels good, good things come to me
I love knowing that when I feel less than good my guidance is telling me that I am not vibrationally ready for the thing that I am contemplating
I appreciate myself for having figured out how my guidance system works
And I am beginning to practice using it more and more
I want to be one who is always tuned in to guidance from Source
I want to be one who follows the path of least resistance
I want to be one who thinks deliberately and acts only when guided to act
I am beginning to understand the perfection of how things work
I am beginning to trust my guidance
I want my guidance to lead me towards making the most of this beautiful day
I want my guidance to take me where I need to go, and do what I need to do and meet who I need to meet in order to feel satisfied with my day.
Thank you Source for always being there with me and guiding me with your love
I love you. I love life.

The word of the day

Joy

www.zmahoon.com

95. Joy

Thank you God for this brand new day.
Thank you for the joy I feel as I wake up this morning
Thank you for the joy I feel as I gaze at my son sleeping soundly beside me
Thank you for the joy I feel as I look out on to the trees in my backyard and the sun rise turning the sky bright pink

I want to feel for joy and find joy through out my day
I want to go about my work joyfully
I want to infect everyone around me with a feeling of joy
I want to radiate joy
I want to feel the feeling of joy make my heart swell
I want to enjoy the food I eat
I want to enjoy the things I do
I want to enjoy my interactions with the people who play with me today
I want to enjoy being in my physical body and feeling it's wellbeing at every level
I want to enjoy mental agility and the feeling of clarity

I love feeling joyful and I want more of that
I want to feel the joy of loving and being loved
I want to feel the joy of all things being easy
I want to feel the joy of knowing my wellbeing
I want to feel the joy of living and just being
I want to feel the joy of being energized
I want to feel the joy of simple little things
Like the pretty coloured flowers, and the birds and squirrels
I want to feel the joy of watching big puffy clouds go by
I want to feel the joy of gazing on beautiful things
I want to feel the joy of abundance and freedom and zest

I want to feel the joy of being alive in every moment of every day
I love knowing that I can turn my attention to joyful things at will
I love knowing that by doing so I create more joy
I want to live in a joyful world
I want to see joy on every face
Thank you for this beautiful joyful day
I love you God. I love life.

Word of the day

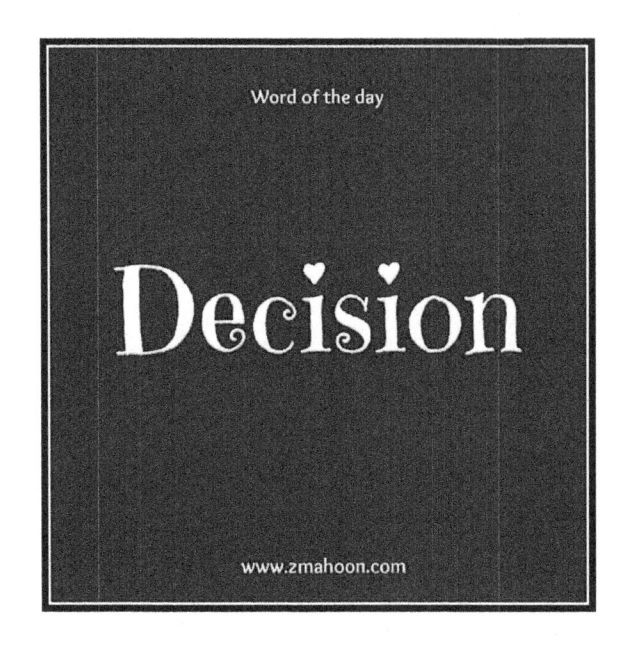

Decision

www.zmahoon.com

96. Decision

Dear God, thank you for another wonderful day
Today I am making the conscious decision to look for things that feel good
I realize that how I allow myself to feel is a decision
And I can always decide how I want to feel in ay moment
Because I can always find a better feeling thought
I realize that with each thought I am making a decision that leads to how I feel that leads to what happens in my life

Today I have decided to be a conscious creator
Today I will pay attention to the way I am thinking my thoughts
Today I will ask myself "how can I say it better?"
Today I will ask myself "what's the best thing I could do right now?"
I know that I can always find better feeling words
I know that I can always find something to do that takes me closer to what I want
I know that when I look for things to appreciate, they will appear

Today I am making the decision to appreciate the beautiful world I live in
I love and appreciate the beauty of the blue sky and the sunshine
The birds that fly and the trees and flowers that add colour and shape and texture
Today I am making the decision to find something to appreciate about each person I visit with
Today I am making the decision to see every one as my equal
I am like everyone else and they are like me – we are all extensions of The Source of all things
When I decide to be an appreciator, it is easy to find things to appreciate
Life is good, people are good
God loves us all and wants us all to thrive

Today I am making the decision to trust God and have faith that things are always working out for me
Today I am making the decision to be open to whatever comes

I understand that my vision is limited and I cannot always see what will come next
I understand that my guidance is always leading me to what is best for me
And so even when things seem not to be working they are working
For whatever happens is for the best
There is no need for me to try and control the outcomes, because things always work out for me

Today I am making the decision to look at things from God's point of view
How would God think about what I am about to say?
What would God think about what I am about to do?
How does God feel about the person I am talking to?
What would God want me to say and do?
God loves and when I make the decision to love I am closest to God
I am making that decision now, in this moment
I am making the decision to send love, to be love
Love is the most important emotion in the world
And I am making the decision to remember that in every moment of my day
I want all my thoughts and actions to be guided by love
Love for myself, love for others, love for this beautiful world and love for God
Thank you God for everything. Thank you for your love.
I love you. I love life.

Word of the day

Align

www.zmahoon.com

97. Align

Dear God thank you for a new day
A day to practice alignment
Today I want to be in alignment with who I truly I am
Today I want to be in alignment with the feeling of love
Today I want to be in alignment with the forces of nature
Today I want to be in alignment with all things that I desire
Being in alignment means simply to feel love and appreciation
So today it is my work to appreciate

I am beginning to understand that the only way for me to achieve alignment is through appreciation
And that only through alignment can I find joy consistently
I am also beginning to understand that the only way for me to understand my alignment is to feel the absence of it
When I know what I don't want, that's when I know with more clarity what I want
I am beginning to understand that the only reason I want material objects and relationships is because I think that by having them I will feel good
So I am beginning to understand that everything in life is to seek that feeling of love, joy and harmony
I know that I can feel good without changing the conditions around me
And today this is my work
My work is to find alignment without wanting anything to change
I believe I can do that for I can always reach for a thought that feels better

Word of the day

Blessings

www.zmahoon.com

98. Blessings

Dear God, thank you for this brand new day
I feel happy and blessed as I wake up in my comfy warm bed
I am blessed to wake up relaxed and refreshed
I love and appreciate the many blessings in my life
I feel blessed to have my beautiful children to enjoy every day
I feel blessed with the love the fills our home and every day of our lives
I feel blessed that my work is just a few minutes away from home
I feel blessed that I enjoy my day at work and that it gives me financial stability
I feel blessed that I work with delightful co-creators who are always helping me and supporting me
I feel blessed that I have the opportunity to teach what I know about the law of attraction
I feel so blessed that many gather to co-create with me every Tuesday for meditation
I feel blessed that I have a wonderful gift to simplify complex ideas so that others my benefit
I feel blessed that I have a gift to articulate clearly
I feel blessed to have my beautiful peaceful house and many comforts to enjoy
I feel blessed that I can keep all my commitments and do my best in every day
I feel blessed with the knowledge that I have gained over the years
I feel blessed with the peace within my heart

I want to feel the love and blessings that God is sending my way every moment of every day
I want the ability to recognize my blessings and follow my guidance
I want to feel love in my heart for all things, people and events in my life

I want to feel blessed at every step of my journey
I want to know my blessings and appreciate them
I know now that appreciation is the key to more blessings
I want more blessings, I want to live a blessed life
I want to start each day feeling blessed and end each day feeling blessed
I want love to fill my heart, I want to share my blessings generously knowing that there is always more
I want ease and flow. I want love. I want prosperity. I want health. I want to know that I am of value. I want to feel my value.
Thank you for all my blessings Dear God. Thank you for this wonderful blessed day.
I love you. I love life.

Word of the day

Relish

zmahoon.com

99. Relish

Dear God, thank you for this beautiful new day
So much to do, so many things to enjoy
So many happy memories to create
So many wonderful things to relish!

I relish in the warmth of the sunshine streaming in through my window
I relish the beauty of the colors of this world as I look out on to it
I relish the trees with their changing colors
I relish how the sunlight falls on them and sets them on fire
I relish at the thought of my perfect mug of morning coffee
I relish the thought of my morning walk with the cool fresh breeze in my face
I relish the thought of spending the day with my children
I relish the thought of the food we'll eat and the things we will do together
I relish their comradery, their laughter and their jokes

Dear God, thank you so much for all these wonderful gifts
Thank you for all the wonderful things I have relished in the past
I relish all the places I've been to and the things I've done
I relish the life I have created for myself
I relish the thought of all the wonderful things I have created that are on their way
I relish thinking about the ways in which they will come
I relish the feeling of freedom I feel today
For today I know that all things really are possible
I relish the feeling of abundance I feel
For I know that there is always more
I relish the feeling of strength and stamina in my body
And I know that my body functions perfectly

I relish my creativity and the creativity of others
For I know that it is the basis for all new things in the world

I relish knowing that I have an important place in the universe
And that my contribution to the world is important
I relish knowing that I am a teacher at my core
And that I can help many find the answers they seek
I relish being a conduit for your work Dear God
Thank you for all my blessings
I love you. I love life.

Word of the day

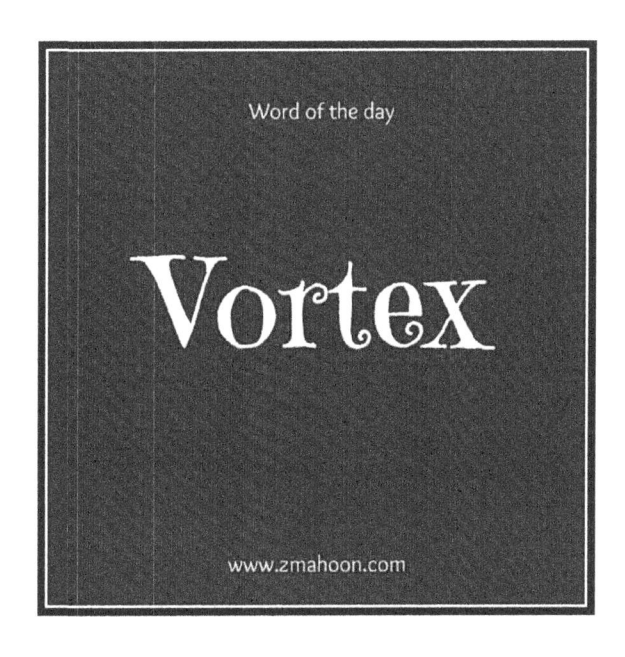

Vortex

www.zmahoon.com

100. Vortex

Dear God, thank you for another wonderful day
So much to look forward to
So much to be thankful for
So many things to enjoy
So much love to share
So much joy to feel
Today I want to be who I am inside my vortex
In my vortex I am a powerful creator
In my vortex I can have, be or do anything I want
In my vortex life feels good
In my vortex I love everyone around me
In my vortex I love life
In my vortex I look out on to the world with curiosity
In my vortex I laugh often and have fun
In my vortex I love nature, trees, animals, birds, flowers
In my vortex I appreciate color
In my vortex I appreciate my eyes that see the beauty of this world
In my vortex my food tastes Oh so good
In my vortex I am relaxed and happy
In my vortex I have everything I need
In my vortex I appreciate contrast as step one of the creation process
In my vortex I allow my guidance to come through
In my vortex I have abundance of all things
In my vortex money flows to me in many different ways
In my vortex I have many friends that I enjoy spending time with
In my vortex I enjoy the work I do and it energizes me
In my vortex I feel satisfied with each day
In my vortex I feel free, to do what I want to do
In my vortex all things are possible

In my vortex I am ready for more
In my vortex I am thriving in every way
In my vortex my body feels good
In my vortex I feel my health and my stamina
In my vortex I find things to appreciate about everything
In my vortex I love myself for who I am and who I am becoming
In my vortex life feels good
In my vortex I love life
I love being in the vortex
And it is my conscious decision to be aware of my thoughts so that I can always find my way to the vortex where everything that I want is
Thank you Dear God, for everything that I have learnt
Thank you for all the teachers who have come to me and helped me along
Thank you for your guidance at every step
Thank you God for everything
I love You, I love life

Prayers from Abraham

abraham-hicks.com

Abraham's morning intention

Abraham has played a pivotal role in my learning and knowing. The prayer produced below is an important part of my journey. There are days when for whatever reason I am unable to write my own prayer, and on those days Abraham's morning intention is what I reach for to set my day off on a positive note. I have this prayer memorized and it is the first thought I offer upon waking up in the morning. Enjoy~

Today no matter where I am going
No matter what I am doing
No matter who I am doing it with
It is my dominant intent
To look for things that feel good

When I feel good
I'm vibrating with my higher power

When I feel good I'm in harmony with
That which I consider to be good

When I feel good
I am in the mode of attracting that which will
please me when it gets here

And when I feel good, I feel good

I'm a powerful creator
I am unlimited
I can have, be or do anything I want

~ Abraham ~
From the book Money and the Law of Attraction by Esther and Jerry Hicks

About the author

Zehra Mahoon lives in Ontario, Canada with her two beautiful children, Kinza and Faris, a hyper cat called Izzy, a lazy cat called Sitka and Stella the forever puppy.

Zehra loves her small town Oshawa and over the past fourteen years she has finally adjusted to the snow and cold weather in Ontario, but always welcomes a timely opportunity to get away to warmer places preferably with lots of old trees, rocks and water, good food and vibrant colours.

Zehra teaches weekly meditation classes at the local library and offers an open discussion session. She loves to teach, coach and write for her blog, as well as other journals and magazines. Zehra is an accomplished speaker and often makes television appearances. Aside from teaching the law of attraction, and offering financial advice , Zehra loves to cook and entertain and have fun with each new day of her life.

To find out more about Zehra and her work please visit her website.

Zehra's other books include:

Thrive – Free yourself from Worry, Anger and other negative emotions

Many books have been written about anger management and over coming worry and anxiety and about what to think and believe and how to act, but three things set this book apart from the rest:

1. The depiction of the thinking process in the form of illustrations that make it easy to understand how our thoughts impact our results; 2. A method that helps us to identify the beliefs that operate under the surface and control our lives without our knowing it; and 3. A simple four step process that helps to deactivate negative beliefs permanently so that we can thrive.

The end result: freedom from worry, anxiety, and anger and a set of thinking exercises that can be used in every situation you would ever encounter in life.

Is this Apple from my Tree? is a book about parenting.

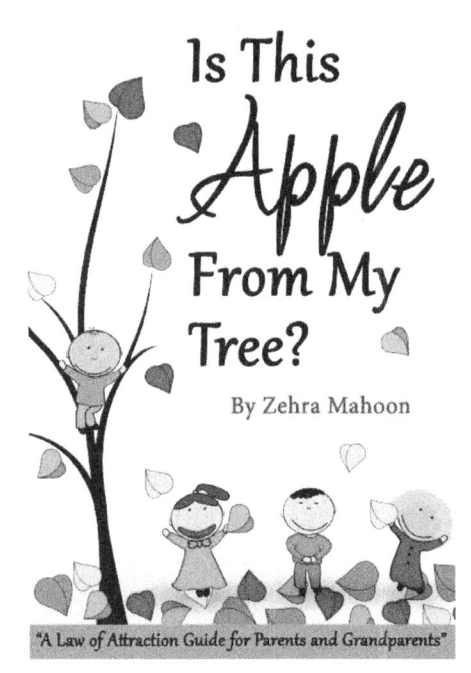

Being a good parent is as much about looking after yourself as it is about looking after your child.

This book will help you to:

1. Become a confident, relaxed and happy parent who enjoys every moment of having children.

2. Raise children with positive belief systems that enable them to be confident, happy, healthy, creative, and successful.

Zehra shares many practical examples of situation that she encountered with her own children how she dealt with them successfully to help you understand how your power of positive thinking impacts your children without ever having to tell them to change or do anything differently.

Peace Within is a book about meditation

Meditation is made out to be way more difficult than it truly is. One of the reasons for this is that there are so many different ways being taught. The purpose of this little book is to dig down to the foundation of the process of meditation and talk about why things are done in various different ways. The fewer the rules and rituals the easier it is.

This book makes meditation easy.

If you have wanted to learn meditation and felt that you could not turn off your thoughts then this book is meant for you for you are about to learn that there is really no need for you to ever turn your thoughts off – in fact you can't – that's the equivalent of telling your heart to stop pumping blood!

The Prosperity Puzzle: Your relationship with money and how to improve it

Have you ever wondered why some people who have the skills and the education and everything else they need to be successful aren't and others who have far less qualifications are?

Have you ever wondered why one business in the same industry with the same product succeeds and another doesn't?

That's what this book is all about – it explains how the way we think about money has an impact upon how much money flows into our lives.

It explains how to work on and remove the negative beliefs that are standing between you and prosperity. You deserve to be rich, and anything that you want is possible.

Win: a law of attraction guide to winning

The Law of Attraction is always working, whether you use it consciously or not.

This powerful law is at the base of why things out the way they do.

This book will help you to improve your understanding of the nine important elements that contribute towards winning anything – especially the lottery, accompanied with step wise guide to making them work for you.

This book will give you an understanding of what you need to stop doing in order to start winning the lottery and so much more.

If thoughts create then... why do bad things happen to good people?

This is a FREE BOOK

The purpose of this book is to explain why bad things happen to good people, and how to learn to control your thought process in order to create a future that you really want to live.

You can download a free pdf copy of this book at www.zmahoon.com

Zehra's books are available in digital and print formats through Amazon.com

101.   One Last Thing...

If you enjoyed this book or found it useful I would truly appreciate it if you would post a short review on Amazon. Your support really does make a difference and I read all the reviews personally so I can get your feedback and make this book even better.
Much love and appreciation,
Zehra

Made in the USA
Coppell, TX
07 February 2022